Get
It
Done
When
You're
Depressed

Get It Done When You're Depressed

50 Strategies for Keeping Your Life on Track

Julie A. Fast and John D. Preston, Psy.D., ABPP

ALPHA

A member of Penguin Group (USA) Inc.

ALPHA BOOKS

Published by the Penguin Group

Penguin Group (USA) Inc., 375 Hudson Street, New York, New York 10014, USA

Penguin Group (Canada), 90 Eglinton Avenue East, Suite 700, Toronto, Ontario M4P 2Y3, Canada (a division of Pearson Penguin Canada Inc.)

Penguin Books Ltd., 80 Strand, London WC2R 0RL, England

Penguin Ireland, 25 St. Stephen's Green, Dublin 2, Ireland (a division of Penguin Books Ltd.)

Penguin Group (Australia), 250 Camberwell Road, Camberwell, Victoria 3124, Australia (a division of Pearson Australia Group Pty. Ltd.)

Penguin Books India Pvt. Ltd., 11 Community Centre, Panchsheel Park, New Delhi—110 017, India

Penguin Group (NZ), 67 Apollo Drive, Rosedale, North Shore, Auckland 1311, New Zealand (a division of Pearson New Zealand Ltd.)

Penguin Books (South Africa) (Pty.) Ltd., 24 Sturdee Avenue, Rosebank, Johannesburg 2196, South Africa

Penguin Books Ltd., Registered Offices: 80 Strand, London WC2R 0RL, England

International Standard Book Number: 978-1-59257-706-4
Library of Congress Catalog Card Number: 2007932654

10   09   08   8   7   6   5   4   3   2   1

Interpretation of the printing code: The rightmost number of the first series of numbers is the year of the book's printing; the rightmost number of the second series of numbers is the number of the book's printing. For example, a printing code of 08-1 shows that the first printing occurred in 2008.

Printed in the United States of America

Note: This publication contains the opinions and ideas of its authors. It is intended to provide helpful and informative material on the subject matter covered. It is sold with the understanding that the authors and publisher are not engaged in rendering professional services in the book. If the reader requires personal assistance or advice, a competent professional should be consulted.

The authors and publisher specifically disclaim any responsibility for any liability, loss, or risk, personal or otherwise, which is incurred as a consequence, directly or indirectly, of the use and application of any of the contents of this book.

Trademarks: All terms mentioned in this book that are known to be or are suspected of being trademarks or service marks have been appropriately capitalized. Alpha Books and Penguin Group (USA) Inc. cannot attest to the accuracy of this information. Use of a term in this book should not be regarded as affecting the validity of any trademark or service mark.

Most Alpha books are available at special quantity discounts for bulk purchases for sales promotions, premiums, fund-raising, or educational use. Special books, or book excerpts, can also be created to fit specific needs.

For details, write: Special Markets, Alpha Books, 375 Hudson Street, New York, NY 10014.

To Laura Solop, with love and appreciation. —Julie

Contents

1 Don't Wait Until You *Want* to Do Something 1

2 Focus Outwardly 7

3 Wait Until You Finish Your Work to Judge It 13

4 Make Your Own Decisions 17

5 Set Up a Realistic Work Space 23

6 Be Your Own Drill Sergeant 29

7 Structure Your Day Like a Child's 33

8 Remind Yourself That You're Depressed 39

9 Eliminate Distractions 43

10 Think Like an Athlete 49

11 Expect Brain Chatter 55

12 Write Yourself a Letter 59

13 Break Through the Depression Barrier 63

14 Feel the Depression … and Do It Anyway 67

15 Finish School 73

16 Talk Back to Depression 79

17 Set Time Limits 83

18 Expect to Be Physically Uncomfortable 87

19 Just Sit Down 91

20 Know When Your Brain Is Lying to You 95

21 Don't Worry About Something, *Do* Something 101

22 Regulate Your Sleep 105

23 Work with a Friend 109

24 Break Projects into Steps 113

25 Ask Someone to Do the Little Stuff for You 117

26 Learn to Say No 121

27 Focus, Focus, Focus. 127

28 Get Ready the Night Before 133

29 Expect to Have Trouble Thinking 137

30 Beware Caffeine and Sugar Highs 143

31 Distinguish Between Depression and Low Self-Esteem 149

32 Avoid Isolation 155

33 Always Do Your Best 159

34 Educate Your Friends and Family About Depression 165

35 Expect to Cry 171

36 Accept the Losses Caused by Depression 175

37 Set Outside Limits 181

38 Get Some Exercise 185

39 Pay to Get the Help You Need 189

40 Tackle One Project at a Time 195

41 Get Help for Anxiety 199

42 Watch What You Say 205

43 See a Therapist 211

44 Accept the Limitations Caused by Depression. 217

45 Explore Medication 223

46 Find Your Work Purpose 229

47 Be Realistic About the Hours in a Week 235

48 Allow Time for Positive Results 239

49 Create Creativity 243

50 Praise Yourself All Day 249

     Conclusion 253

     Index 257

Introduction

When you read my bio in the back of this book and see my career accomplishments, you might think I no longer have depression and that must be why I can write and work successfully. Unfortunately, that's not the case. I'm still depressed more than I'm well. However, the key is that I've learned to work through my depression instead of letting my depression rob me of my ability to work or otherwise get things done. In reality, I can only work about half the time other people work. I can't do a 9-to-5 job, and I get worn out if I spend too much time focusing on a large project. As a result, I have had to learn to be much more productive when I work.

I have had to teach myself certain strategies, which I outline for you in the following pages, for working through my depression enough to function, enough to get things done even when I'm depressed. Once I freed myself from the limitations of depression, I was able to create a system that works for me. Depression may take over my mind, but it doesn't have to take over my actions. I have a lot of tough days, and I would love to have depression out of my life permanently, but until then, I'll continue to use the strategies in this book to get things done.

You *Can* Change Your Life

Getting things done forms the basis of your daily life. You constantly have to take care of yourself and others (family, friends, pets), work, eat, drive, create, collaborate, meet deadlines, make decisions, give and receive love, tend to your health, manage your money, and so very much more. And all this takes energy. But depression robs you of this energy—and along with it, often strips away the hope and belief that you'll ever get it back. That's why it's so essential that you have a plan in place for getting things done despite your down mood. I've been there; I know what you're going through. And the good news is, I have a plan that will help you.

As impossible as it sounds, and no matter how depressed you are, you *can* create a plan to get things done when you're depressed. It isn't easy, and it takes time to create your own system, but it's worth it when you can get into bed at night and feel good about yourself and what you've accomplished. When you think of your options—getting things done versus quitting jobs, rarely finishing projects, always feeling guilty and sad, and in general not believing in your own abilities—the choice is clear. You want to get things done. The strategies in this book help you do just that.

Explore Your Depression History

Before you get started with the strategies in this book, it helps to explore a few areas to really uncover the role depression plays and has played in your life. Life has a way of getting away from you when you're depressed. By realistically examining your past, you can have a better idea of what you want for your future.

First, think about what happens when you don't get things done. Which of the following problems have you experienced due to depression?

- ☐ Relationship problems
- ☐ Lack of self-confidence
- ☐ Wondering why things are so hard for you while they seem so effortless for others
- ☐ Looking back on your life and feeling shame at all the time you've wasted

Now think about what others say to you. Put a check next to the comments that sound familiar:

- ☐ "If you just sat down and did it, you wouldn't have so many problems."
- ☐ "You have a family. It seems to me that you should work harder to make sure they're okay."
- ☐ "God! It's just doing the dishes!"
- ☐ "You have so much talent. It's a shame that you just waste it."

Perhaps most important when you're batting depression, as we can sometimes be our own harshest critic, think about what you say to yourself. Put a check next to the following that you've thought or said:

- ☐ "I'll never get my act together. I've been like this for so long. I can't see anything changing soon."

☐ "I just don't know what I want to do! If I knew that, I would just do it instead of sitting around."

☐ "I really want to change, but it's like all the air goes out of my balloon as soon as I sit down to do something."

The effects of depression can seem endless. They can affect your life in every area and make you feel that things will *never* get better. And unfortunately, some people don't see depression as an illness and can say hurtful things. But the main problem is how you treat yourself. When depression takes over and you say the same hurtful things to yourself as others say to you, it's difficult to get better. When you start getting things done, that negative self-talk can turn into more positive talk, and that's just what you need.

Getting It Done Isn't Just About Work

Most of us have to work to earn a paycheck to support ourselves and our family. But working is only part of what you have to do during the day, and only one of the many things that might feel utterly impossible to accomplish when you're depressed.

The saying "Start where you are" is very useful here. For some people, getting things done really does mean getting out of bed in the morning and at least going through the motions of the day. For others, it may be finishing work projects or studying for an exam. You just have to get started doing something. Chances are, that something will lead to something else, and so on, and before you know it, you'll have a few things checked off your to-do list.

Depression Is Physiological

Picture this scenario: your partner walks into your room and sees you lying in bed, crying. He walks up to you and puts his hand on your head.

"You're burning up!" he says. Then he hears you cough. "Oh no! That sounds terrible. You need to go to the doctor."

"No, I'm not that bad," you say. "I just need to rest and get better."

"What are you talking about? This is dangerous! You might have pneumonia. I'm taking you to the emergency room right now."

Now picture this scenario: your partner walks into your room and sees you lying in bed, crying.

"What's wrong?" he asks. "Why are you still in bed? It's so dark in here! You really need to get up and do something. You've missed work three days this week!"

You start to cry and say, "I just can't seem to get better. I don't want to live like this anymore."

"I don't know how to help you," he says, scared and/or frustrated. "I don't know what you need. You just need to get up so you can get better!"

You continue to lie there, filled with despair because you don't have the energy or the desire to get up. He walks out of the room ....

Even though it's often not seen this way, depression is a physiological illness that needs to be treated as compassionately and as successfully as any physical illness. No matter whether your depression is the result of a certain, recent event or if your depression has been around for years, the fact is that your brain is not functioning correctly. You need to do all you can to get better, just as you would if you had pneumonia or some other physical illness.

How the Strategies in This Book Work

You already know you're depressed, and you're probably trying to get better in a variety of ways, but what do you do while you're trying and the depression is still around? You take action. That's what this book is about—taking action—and that's what the strategies in this book help you do. The strategies help with work, home life, school, and relationships, enabling you to take action even when that feels impossible. When you take action and fight back, you can get things done—you just need tools that are stronger than depression.

There's a person without depression inside you. This is the real you, the you outside the illness. The strategies in this book teach you to override depression so you can act like the real you, the person who *can* get things done. This is never easy, as the illness may have dictated your behavior for many years, but change—and sometimes extreme change—*is* possible.

About the Stories

The stories in this book represent the personal histories of people with depression as told to the authors. The names and some details such as gender and profession have been changed to protect the teller's privacy. In some instances, what's printed is a composite of stories told by more than one person.

The "My Story" features have *not* been changed. Julie is very open about her own depression and the many mistakes she has made while learning to manage this illness successfully.

A Final Note

Get It Done When You're Depressed is not a depression treatment book, although it can be used as a companion to any other professional and personal treatments you're currently using. But there's no question that once you implement the strategies in this book and become more productive, your depression can definitely lessen. For some, it may go away completely. But for those whose depression treatment is ongoing or has not yet responded to other treatments, this book can be used as an integral part of an overall treatment strategy.

Getting things done is one of the best ways to feel better about yourself, which is automatically an antidote to depression. When you can go to bed feeling better than when you woke up, that's an accomplishment you can be proud of.

Don't Wait Until You *Want* to Do Something

Many people equate depression with the *inability* to work. In reality, the problem is often the inability to *feel* like working. People who are depressed assume that their lack of motivation is a sign of weakness, and if they could just buck up a bit, they would be more productive.

But waiting until you feel like doing something is the single biggest mistake you can make when you're depressed and need to get things done. Working when you think you can't is one of the main difficulties you may face when you're depressed, which is why you have to be ready to work no matter how you feel.

This Will Feel All Wrong

There's a big difference between the great feeling of motivation that comes when you want to do a project and the lack of motivation you feel when you wake up feeling down with low energy. It's natural that when you *feel* motivated, you can get things done more easily and feel a sense of accomplishment while you work. When you're depressed you often lack motivation, so as much as you might want to feel the desire to work, it simply isn't there.

But for some good news: when you simply get started with something, you begin to feel more motivated and find it easier to do what you have to do. This can help end the pattern of continually searching for something that makes you feel more excited instead of just moving forward with a project no matter how you feel.

Do you recognize any of the following signs that you need to work anyway?

- You believe that lack of motivation is a sign you *can't* work.
- You've decided that there's no use in starting if you don't have the desire for a project.

- You search for the feeling of wanting to get something done even when you know that lack of motivation is a normal symptom of depression.
- You wait so long to get a good feeling about what you need to do that you never even get started.

If you see your thoughts in any of these, you might be able to use this as your jumping-off point to get started with something.

Alice's Story

I've learned something in the past year. Depression never wants to do anything. *Ever.* I used to wonder why everything seemed so impossible. I saw other people get excited about their work and just assumed they were in the right profession and I wasn't.

I've always loved to paint. When I got depressed in the past, I would quit painting entirely. There were no ideas and I had no desire to get started on anything. I was sure my work would never be as good simply because I didn't enjoy it as much. I used to feel totally blank when I knew I had to create something. I missed a lot of years because of this. I think of all of the wonderful art I could have now. It's sad.

One day a friend asked me something interesting: "Alice, have you ever painted something when you were depressed?" "Yes," I said. "And is the work as good as the work you do when you're well?" I thought about it and realized that in terms of the work itself, I couldn't tell the difference between my well work and my depressed work. Then she said, "The problem isn't your ability to work; the problem is that you want to feel excited about the work before you start."

She was totally right. Instead of focusing on the art and what it would look like when it was done, I focused on the upfront feeling that I couldn't do something because I was lacking so much of the desire I usually felt. I now paint no matter how much I feel. I cry a lot while I'm painting sometimes, but that's fine.

My Story

I've always thought motivation was the reason people got things done better than I did. I remember going into a project with a small desire to finally get something done. That lasted for a while and then I would suddenly feel that desire slip away, and only a feeling of hopelessness would remain. So I constantly quit things and tried something else. I changed jobs, put off cleaning my house, stopped calling friends, and everything else that *felt* impossible.

Today, for example, I make myself pick up the phone when I'm depressed, even when something that simple feels impossible. I'm so thankful for the days I do feel motivated—they're like a gift. I can't stress enough the fact that I no longer wait until the days when life is more normal and I do feel motivated. I would *never* get anything done if I did that. I'm often amazed at how much I enjoy the work once I get started.

What I do now:

- After years of waiting for the elusive good feeling that comes with wanting to do something, I finally accepted the fact that I've never wanted to do certain things when I'm depressed and I never will. So I try to do them anyway.

- I focus on the outcome instead of how I feel when I start.

- I ask myself, *How will I feel when I go to bed if I don't do something?*

- I know there will be many days when the depression is stronger than I am. I keep going anyway and wait for the wonderful feeling of motivation to finally show up. If it never does, at least I have accomplished something.

Exercise

Look over the following statements and decide if they are true or false:

- When you're depressed, you can only get things done when you get the feeling that the time is right.
- You have to know what you want before you can go for it.
- When there's no motivation, there's no way to move forward.
- Other people have more motivation, which is why they can do more than you can.
- Not wanting to do something is a sign that you need to do something different.

How many of these statements do you think are true? You might be surprised to learn that they're *all false*. You'll always want to feel desire, motivation, joy, and a sense of accomplishment when you do a project, but the reality is that this might never happen when you're depressed. You just have to do the work anyway.

ASK DR. PRESTON

Q **Why do so many people wait to do something until they feel like doing something and then feel really terrible when they don't get anything done?**

A Lots of life's tasks aren't especially rewarding. They're tedious or difficult, and most people motivate themselves to do these things by consciously anticipating how they'll feel when the task is accomplished. These people are able to internally generate the drive and energy to get started.

Depressed people, on the other hand, find it very hard to ignite this self-generated action due, in large part, to decreased metabolic functioning in the frontal lobes of their brain, which are responsible for initiating behavior. So if a person waits to feel the desire to get started, he or she might wait a long time and not only *not* accomplish the nonrewarding tasks but also miss out on the big projects that can bring big rewards.

You Have More Control Than You Think

You can create a feeling of motivation and desire to do something by starting it first and then waiting for the feelings to arrive—and they often do. Of all the strategies in this book, this one might be the most important in terms of getting started with a project. This strategy can form a foundation for you to get things done when you're depressed.

Here are some other thoughts to consider:

- Accept that motivation may never come when you're depressed, but you can do the work anyway.

- Keep working until you do feel even a small sense of accomplishment, and hold on to that as you finish a project.

- Work no matter what so you can go to bed with a sense of accomplishment.

- Remember, lack of motivation and desire are a very normal part of depression.
- Start, start, start. The motivation often shows up.

Remember: Depression doesn't want to do anything and never will. It's an inert illness, not an active illness. If you wait until you "feel like it" to start something, you'll wait forever!

2

Focus Outwardly

Depression is a very selfish illness that makes you focus internally all the time. Everything is about *you*, whether you want it to be or not—*your* rotten feelings, *your* bad thoughts, *your* inferior performance. This is a natural and unfortunate part of depression, and it's very counter-productive to getting things done. Projects at work and at home often involve collaboration, and when you're focused on what *you* feel and what *you're* doing wrong, it's very frustrating for the people you're with, who might see you as a burden or too annoying to work with.

This is especially true if you're lethargic *and* very negative. When you're depressed, it's hard to take interest in what's going on around you, which further isolates you from the people in your life who might be able to help you get things done if you weren't so difficult to be around. This can happen with work, family, friends, and any other situation where you have to work with others. And it has to be noticed and stopped, or it can severely limit your work and social relationships.

Change Starts with You

By recognizing negative, internal, annoying, or whiny behavior in your-self, you can use that self-knowledge to make a change for the better. You *can* be depressed and be nice. You *can* be depressed and think of others. In fact, when you stop the negative behavior your depression is causing, you might be more honest with the people in your life, especially your co-workers, and ask for their help to keep you on a positive track.

Focusing on things outside yourself can be very difficult, and you might easily find yourself getting caught in the web of negative internal dialogue and lack of consciousness. The more you listen to what you say and realize what you do when you're depressed, the easier it will be for you to look around you and become a positive and productive part of the world again, even when you're depressed.

Do you recognize any of the following selfish behaviors you engage in when you're depressed?

- You constantly focus on depression even when things around you are positive.

- You're unable to notice what's going on around you to the point that you miss seeing when other people are upset.

- You neglect others, including your family, to dwell on your depression.

- Others regard you as selfish, annoying, and constantly complaining.

Recognition is the first and most powerful step. When you catch yourself focusing inwardly, you can open up and make different behavioral choices.

Kate's Story

I used to have a very bad reputation at work. When I felt down, I let people know how unhappy I was. I didn't realize it was depression, and I certainly didn't see the pattern of my selfishness. I would get to work and just be so low that I felt I couldn't get out of my chair. I literally couldn't get out of my head and how terrible I felt. People started to avoid me, and I know they thought I was Jekyll and Hyde. On some days I could be outgoing and participate, and on others, I was like a selfish little baby.

One day, a co-worker who was obviously very frustrated (or very compassionate) came into my office and told me she'd had enough of my moping. I'm not kidding. I started to cry and told her I was having trouble with depression. I'm lucky because she understood. She said, "I have tough days, too, but I always have to remember I'm part of a group. I always think of the group on my bad days."

This was good advice. When I'm mildly depressed, which is often, I think of the group instead of staying in my head and feeling sorry for myself.

My Story

I once had a therapist tell me I was the most selfish depressed person she had met in a long time. This was a therapist I knew very well and greatly respected, so I was understandably shocked and very upset at first. I went home and cried—a lot. I thought, *But I'm depressed all the time. I can't help it! I can't do anything about it!*

I was at a point in my life when my sitting around crying and not being able to even get out of the house had gone on long enough.

I really thought about what she said. If it was true—and I realized it was—how was it affecting my ability to do what I wanted in life? Was I really that selfish? I thought about how I talked with others and how well I was doing at my part-time job, and I was pretty appalled. I talked about my health a lot and often had trouble doing my work.

I knew that wanting to change was a good start. I tried to be more aware of how I fit in with people at my job. I just did things instead of having a running commentary about them. People noticed. It was a relief for me because I could focus on helping my depression instead of wallowing in it. This helped my work, too.

What I do now:

- I'm very, very aware of how negative I used to be, and now I don't let it go very far. If it does, I always say, "I'm sorry. I'm feeling very negative today, and I don't want to take it out on you!" This always works and helps me calm down.

- When depression makes me feel completely isolated and lonely, I know it's not always as real as it seems. I try not to let myself really go inward and write in my journal all night about how sick I am. Instead, I call someone and try to connect with the outside world.

- I'm truly aware of how my behavior affects others and how my words add to a conversation. I want what I say and do to reflect who I am, not what depression makes me seem. I look for signals that I'm not exactly being pleasant.

Exercise

Read over the following prompts and answer in terms of how well you got things done this week. If that wasn't an issue, answer about your behavior in general.

List five things you did this week that were selfish, inward thinking, and possibly annoying to others because you were depressed:

1. _____
2. _____
3. _____

4. _____

5. _____

List five things you did this week that helped others, added to a conversation, or made someone feel good:

1. _____

2. _____

3. _____

4. _____

5. _____

Your goal is to have more entries in the positive section, even when you're depressed. That's true for this week, and next week, and for the rest of your life.

ASK DR. PRESTON

Q

Why is depression so selfish?

A

Any kind of intensely painful experience causes people to become more self-centered (at least temporarily). This is true for high states of emotional distress as well as for physical pain. It's hard to worry about starving children in Africa when you feel like your whole world is crumbling. Plus, talking (sharing, feeling understood, being cared about) feels comforting, even when the feelings are very negative. The need for the depressed person to process experiences and have people show concern for them likely underlies some of this tendency. Finally, some of the cognitive changes that occur with depression freeze people in the moment; it's what some have called a loss of temporal perspective. As a result, people are focused on the emotions of the moment and are less able to back off from it and see a broader perspective. In other words, it might be harder for depressed people to see the world around them.

Open Up and Look Outside Yourself

When you feel depression start to close in and you feel yourself getting defensive, isolated, whiny, weepy, or complaining, remember to look outward and think of others besides yourself. You can be honest and ask for help instead of keeping it all inside.

If this feels difficult and you really do need to vocalize your symptoms, as many people do, this is a good time to find a compassionate therapist so you can focus on more outwardly positive talk when you're around friends, family, and colleagues.

Here are some other thoughts to consider:

- Talk positively about others and the task at hand, even if it feels impossible. Keep negative self-talk to yourself.

- Ask questions even when you're not feeling interested about any-thing. This helps you generate interest in things around you.

- Ask yourself, *Who am I thinking about right now? Am I only focused on how bad I feel?*

Remember: It's terribly hard to think outwardly when you're depressed—it can feel like having to sing when you have laryngitis. But you *must* do it.

Wait Until You Finish Your Work to Judge It

Depression is a harsh judge. It tells you that you rarely do anything right. No matter what you write; who you call; what you create; or how you give a speech, clean your house, plan a party, or do anything that has a specific result, depression judges you harshly before you can even finish a project. And if you feel that your work isn't up to par, you might quit the project in the middle—or not even start it at all.

This is a natural response to the pressures the judgmental side of depression can put on you. Judging what you do is a quick way to either not start a project at all or stop in the middle to avoid the very unpleasant feelings that you're going to do an inferior job.

Wait Until the End to Judge

When you ignore the internal critic until the end of a project, you at least can complete some projects. You'll probably want to quit many times over, but quitting would mean you're giving in to the fake judge, not your real judge—you. When you're depressed, it can even be hard to think of what you do well. But it's essential that you remind yourself—constantly, if necessary—that you can wait and realistically decide how well you did a project when it's complete.

Learning to be an objective judge of your own work when you're depressed may be one of the most difficult strategies in this book you take on. Depression is a very negative and unforgiving illness. It's ruthless in how it makes you put yourself down for being inadequate when you want to complete projects. By taking over from depression and judging your work realistically, you can recover much of the control depression takes from your life.

Have you had these thoughts while trying to get something done?

- *I'm not doing a very good job on this project.*
- *This is going to turn out really terrible.*

- *This work will be rejected.*
- *Other people would do this much better than I can.*
- *I can't keep going with this.*

When you at least know these thoughts are often unreal, you can better ignore them and just keep going with your project.

James's Story

I taught English in Japan for a few years. I enjoyed the work and especially enjoyed creating ESL (English as a second language) curriculum, but I often struggled with the depression I'd had since I was a teenager. About one year into my stay, I was asked to train a large group of Japanese ESL teachers. At first I wasn't sure I could do it, but I decided what the heck and wrote up a plan.

When I got there, I was amazed to see more than 100 women teachers in the audience, all looking at me expectantly. Then the thoughts started: *You aren't prepared enough. It's always like this, James. You think you can do something and then you take on too much and make a mess. You remember what it's been like in the past. Nothing but mistakes. You're sweating like a pig.* It was at this point that I really started to sweat—just from these negative thoughts! I felt the dark cloud come over me in a wave. It was just a familiar despair that once again I was stopped from doing something I loved.

But this time I kept going and started to teach. I worried throughout the presentation that no one was really listening and that they were bored, but I decided to focus on myself and what I was doing in the moment. I didn't get an emotional break the whole time I was onstage; I just kept going. When I was done, I was proud. When the judgment language resumed, trying to tell me what I'd done wrong, I focused instead on what I'd done correctly. I looked to the people in the audience for judgment. They were talking excitedly, and some came up to me and said they learned a lot. If I had listened to the harsh depression critic like I used to, the experience would have been terrible no matter how well I had done. When I'm depressed, it's better for me to get my reactions from the people on the outside instead of listening to what's going on inside.

My Story

As I write this, I have these thoughts: *This book makes no sense. People will see through my writing and know that it's all terrible. I will be seen as a fraud because I'm no good. This book will be rejected*

14

by my publisher. The editors will think, "Good God, we made a mistake here!" I have the thoughts that everything I do is subpar. I think, *This has all been written before—who am I to think I have something to say?*

Even writing down these thoughts is stressful because I can see how they affected my work so much in the past. I was never able to fight these terribly judgmental thoughts, which is the main reason I never—and I mean *never*—finished big writing projects before I changed my perspective and stopped letting depression define my work. Now I wait until I have the *finished* project in my hand before I judge it. I have never once looked at a finished project and said, "This is no good. I'm no good." I'm always proud that I just finished something.

What I do now:

- I've learned to save my own judgment until the project is finished. I remind myself that I've written quite a few books in the past, and despite the constant depression critic, they have turned out fine.

- I know I must focus on holding the book in my hand instead of how hard it is to deal with the depression thoughts when I'm actually writing the book.

- When the judging thoughts come up, I remind myself, *It's always like this, Julie. It's a sign that you're on track because you always feel this way in the middle of a project.*

Exercise

What project are you working on now that's causing you problems? Or on what daily or weekly project do you constantly judge yourself as inferior? List one example project here:

_____

Write what the judging voice says in the middle of the project here. You can probably come up with plenty of examples.

_____

_____

_____

Now, ask yourself what part of this language is actually from your life—from your childhood, from others, or from you truly not doing the job well. Then ask yourself what part of this is ridiculous and purely the depression judge talking.

ASK DR. PRESTON

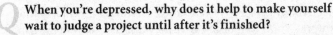

When you're depressed, why does it help to make yourself wait to judge a project until after it's finished?

Ongoing negative appraisals feed the fires of low self-esteem and powerlessness. This is a hallmark of depression. It's always helpful to try to suspend judgment and just focus on what you are doing. Tell yourself, *In this moment, I'm doing the best I can.*

Depression Judgment Is Subjective

Of course, sometimes your work might not be your best, and you might realize this in the middle of a project. In this situation, your thoughts are usually backed up by facts, which means you can make changes and keep going.

On the other hand, the depressed brain makes subjective judgments that can't be backed up by facts. Depression never critiques a project objectively. Impartial, kind, and realistic judgment is best made after you've done your work and the project is over.

Here are some other thoughts to consider:

- Keep going no matter what you hear.
- Focus on the process while you're working.
- Answer the critical thoughts by telling yourself, *I'm willing to just see what will happen. There is no need to get upset now.*

Remember: The projects you judge harshly in the middle usually turn out just fine and look and feel as good as the projects you can easily do when you're well.

Make Your Own Decisions

Have you ever felt so depressed that it seemed impossible to decide on anything, even something as simple as what to have for dinner? Depression takes away your ability to make decisions. Due to chemical changes that take place in your brain when you're depressed, decisions you can normally make without thinking twice can become Herculean tasks. You can often feel panicked, afraid, and worried simply because of the fact that you have to make a decision. Considering how many decisions you have to make in a day, not being able to make even the simplest of decisions is a real problem.

You Versus Your Brain

When you're depressed and have to make a choice about something, there's a good chance that your brain will put up a fight. It's as though your brain is always trying to negotiate for something different from what you want to do. You might struggle with making a decision so much that you wind up confused and tired—and with nothing decided at all. And while you're going through all that, you might miss many positive opportunities to get out and feel better.

Plus, depression can create strong feelings of guilt over what decision you eventually make. This guilt can make you very uncomfortable because you think that either someone is going to get hurt or something is going to be missed as a result of your decision. This feeling can be so stressful you may feel it's easier not to make decisions at all. Unfortunately, this route simply leads back to more depression for not having made a decision.

But you can make your own decisions when you're depressed. Ask yourself what decision you would make if you weren't depressed. If that's not possible, override the pointless back-and-forth with your brain by making a decision, whether or not you like the decision, and then move forward. You might then have to deal with the voice of the depression telling you you've made the wrong choice, but that's easier to deal with than the sense of uselessness that can come from not making a decision at all.

Do you have trouble making any of these kinds of decisions?

- What, when, and where to eat.
- What work project to start on first.
- Where to drive once you get in the car.
- Whether to stay in a relationship.
- Whether to go to a social event.
- When to clean the house.

People are bombarded with decisions daily. Whether these decisions are large or small, overriding depression and making a choice is what matters.

Mike's Story

I can remember being so depressed that I would just drive in circles because I couldn't decide where to go. It was terrible. Then I decided I would drive in one direction toward where I wanted to go—no more getting in the car just to drive aimlessly. When my brain said, *Wrong direction, Mike!* I drove anyway. One time I stood on a street corner and turned in all four directions; it seemed so impossible to decide which direction to turn that I just stood there like a statue. And it drives me crazy when people tell me I should get outside and just do something to feel better when I'm depressed. I often feel so confused as to what I want to do that I do a little bit of everything. But nothing ever feels good.

After years of this, I decided it was time for me to take charge of this situation and to realize that making a choice is actually easy if I just *make* one. It never feels right at first, but I always feel better after I do it.

My Story

For many years I had so much trouble making decisions that it really upset people around me and made it difficult for me to get anything done with pleasure. No matter what I did, my brain told me it was the wrong choice. I would choose one dish in a restaurant, and immediately I knew I should have taken the other one. I'd decide to do something on the weekend, and my brain would say, *Everyone else is doing something different—you made the wrong decision!* When it was really bad, it felt impossible for me to make a decision at all. After going through this for years, one day I just said, *Enough. I'm going to make a decision and stick to it no matter what. I'm so tired of letting depression control my decisions.*

When I write, I have many decisions to make—how to structure the book, what language to use, what audience to target, etc. If I let myself get overwhelmed with these decisions, I lose writing time and feel terrible. Instead, I often let the decisions work themselves out so I can simply function enough to write.

What I do now:

- I remind myself, *Depression won't make a decision today, but I will.*

- I tell myself, *Depression tells me I made the wrong decision, but I didn't. I made a choice, and it's my own.*

- I promise myself I'll choose something no matter what— even when my brain feels so dead I can hardly walk, and even when the guilt makes enjoyment impossible at first.

- I make it clear to myself that I won't analyze my decisions. No second-guessing. Yes, there may be something better, but I've made my decision and I stick to it.

- I always tell myself, *Good for you, Julie!* when I make a decision.

Exercise

It helps if you have some predetermined decisions you can turn to when certain common situations come up, such as the following:

Difficult Decision	Predetermined Decision
Should I go to a party I want to go to?	There is no arguing. If I'm not too tired, I will always go.
Where should I go for lunch?	Let other people decide, and never try to change their decision.

What difficult decisions do you routinely have trouble making? List them in here and then list the set-in-stone decision you can use each time this situation comes up and you're depressed.

Difficult Decision	Predetermined Decision
_____	_____
_____	_____

ASK DR. PRESTON

Q **Why is it so hard to make a decision when you're depressed?**

A There are two things happening here. One has to do with a pervasive sense of not trusting your own judgment. When you're not depressed, you can make many decisions that are accompanied by a feeling of confidence (*I feel confident that this is a good choice*), but during depression, self-doubts predominate.

Also, when you're depressed, you have a greater tendency to primarily see the negative, even in decision-making. A decision such as choosing a restaurant can have some positive elements but also some negative elements. When you're depressed, you're more likely to interpret this choice as exclusively negative.

A Depressed Brain Is a Confused Brain

It's difficult to make a decision when your choices are clouded by depression. By overriding your ill brain and making a decision no matter how it feels, you can calm your thoughts to the point that you can actually enjoy your decision. Once you get used to this process, you can face choices with a plan and always be confident that you know what choice to make.

Here are some other thoughts to consider:

- Let other people pick restaurants, what movie to see, and anything else you find difficult when you're depressed.

- You decide what you do at work. Pick something and do it. Period.

- If you have to make decisions that directly affect other people, remember the type of decisions you make when you're well and copy them when you're depressed.

- Put off big life decisions when you're depressed so you can focus on the smaller, everyday decisions. You can focus on the big decisions later, when you're not depressed.

Remember: Never negotiate with depression. When in doubt and overwhelmed with choices, make one decision. Do it—don't analyze it—and stick to it!

Set Up a Realistic Work Space

Depression can make you feel uncomfortable no matter where you try to work. Maybe you move around all day, trying to find the perfect place that feels right. Or maybe you're too easily distracted by the goings-on around you. No matter your situation, if you're not comfortable in your work space, you're not likely to get things done when you're depressed.

Feeling fidgety or distracted in your work space is a normal part of depression. You can have the feeling that you'd do better if your desk were different or you had more cabinets for your files. And when you have work to do at home, you can feel like moving furniture or buying something new so you can work more effectively. In fact, there's a chance you won't feel comfortable working anywhere.

Choices

Only you know what helps you get things done. Is it a totally clutter-free desk? Do you need music to work by or complete silence? Does it need to be cold or warm? If you can't focus on anything when you need to work, you have to locate yourself someplace where you are able to focus. Look at your choices, pick a place, and most importantly, stick to it. When you want to get up, remind yourself, *This is where I'm working.* It might never feel 100 percent right, but you have to stay put and get your work done.

It's important that you create a work space that accommodates your depression. You have to set up this space on your good days so when you're not having a good day, you can sit down and do what you need to do without worrying about the location or the feel of where you work. Knowing what works for you is the first step; the next is creating the space. The final step is sticking to the space when you need to get something done.

Do you have any of these work space worries?

- Stuck in a cubicle.
- Working from home, which can make you feel isolated and lonely.

- Too many distractions.
- You work in an office and would much prefer to work at home.
- Wrong size chair and table.
- Not enough space.
- Work space is too messy.

It's important that you learn to distinguish between what is truly a work space problem and what uncomfortable feelings are simply a result of depression. When you decide this, you can find a space that really works for you.

Milo's Story

I've worked with computers all my professional life. I always liked the work, but I really hated going in to the office. On the days I felt down, I had to drag myself in on a time schedule that didn't fit my sleep cycle. I was constantly tired and frustrated. I worked in a small cubicle that was more like a box with no windows. I felt like I was going to scream some days.

I actually do better when I have work choices, especially on the days when I don't feel up to meeting people. Asking to telecommute was one of the smartest things I did. I still have to do the same amount of software engineering work, but it's in my home office and on my schedule. I get to look out on my backyard, and I always feel better when I see my trees and hammock. Plus, my dog keeps me company.

My Story

When I'm well, I can pretty much sit and work anywhere. But when I'm depressed, I'm constantly trying to find a comfortable work space. I don't like to write at home, because I feel too isolated. I have trouble at coffee shops simply because I have too many papers to spread out, and I feel guilty for being there too long when I only have one cup of coffee. I've rented office space, gone to the library, and tried to find a group where I can sit and work with other people, but I've never found anything permanent. My main problem is loneliness while I work. I can handle noise, but it's the quiet I don't like.

I'm still searching. I wrote part of this book in a nice space with brick walls and interesting pictures on the wall, but I felt like I was in a void without human contact. At the library, I feel that

I'm isolated because all around me people are reading or studying in small groups and I'm writing alone.

What I do now:

- I face the fact that I simply cannot write if I have access to my e-mail. I have to work in a place with no Internet connection. This is getting harder and harder due to wireless.

- I know that I'm never really comfortable anywhere when I'm not feeling my best, so I have to forget the idea that there is one perfect workspace for me out there and the notion that I'll find it if I just keep looking! It's not going to happen. I have to find the most comfortable place I can and just sit down and work.

Exercise

Think about the problems you currently have with your work environment and answer these questions:

What do I dislike about my environment?

_____

_____

What are three simple changes I can make in the next few days?

_____

_____

What do I need to change in my environment to help me get things done in a timely manner with the least amount of stress?

_____

_____

Who can help me with this?

_____

_____

How can I keep it going?

_____

_____

Where am I most productive?

_____

_____

What are my options, considering my current situation?

_____

_____

What is the best work environment I've ever experienced?

_____

_____

Now use this information to create a space where you can really work, and stick to it!

ASK DR. PRESTON

 Why is it often so hard for a depressed person to find a comfortable place to work?

 Because depressed people have trouble maintaining attention and concentration, lots of places may seem too distracting. Maybe you anticipate that it won't be conducive to productive work, and that may be accurate. Or maybe, while depressed, you, like many other depressed people, have a general state of pessimism, with little energy and motivation and a mental state that predicts failure or frustration. In such cases, almost any environment could seem like it isn't suitable.

Stop the Constant Search

Constantly searching for a comfortable place to work can take a lot of your time. By planning ahead and finding or creating a space that fits your style, you can feel more comfortable and the work can flow more easily. On the other hand, if you can't find a space that feels right, do the best you can and know that you'll be more comfortable on better days.

Consider these suggestions from others:

- I have to have a clean desk, an aromatherapy candle, a printer, and a cup of ice.
- I need my children to be in the other room and, if possible, completely out of the house.
- I have to get out of the house. Being alone makes me more depressed. I work in noisy coffee shops when I have a paper due.
- I shut the door at my office and put a "Working, available in two hours" sign on my door. People actually respect this.
- I go to the library and work in a small room with no Internet access. I turn off my phone and force myself to work.
- I telecommute.
- I make jewelry and hate arranging my beads. I now make jewelry for a woman in trade for her coming in and cleaning my work space every two weeks.

Remember: When you have a project due or especially work that requires sitting, think of the environment that makes it easier to get this done and create or find that environment. If you can't find a place that feels comfortable, remind yourself that you have to choose a location anyway. Once there, stay put, work, and don't change your mind.

6

Be Your Own Drill Sergeant

People with depression use many different techniques to manage the illness, and it's important that you know which techniques work for you. For some, a soft approach is needed. For others, tough love is more helpful. Even if you're the type who responds well to softer language, you probably have days when talking to yourself in a kind and gentle way just won't work. It might be that the depression won't lift and getting things done is impossible, even if you use a certain approach that's helped in the past. These are the days when you have to step aside and let someone or something else take over. Sometimes you need to call upon your inner drill sergeant and let him or her take over and get you back on track. This takes imagination and a willingness to be slightly silly, but you can do it.

Drill Sergeants Don't Mess Around

Wouldn't it be nice on your depressed days if you had someone behind you saying, *Get up out of that bed, soldier! Get dressed and look good and get in your car! I said get in your car! What do you think this is, Club Med? You have work to do, and I expect you to do it! And enjoy doing it! Now drive to work, or whatever else you need to do, and get on with your day! Enough of this time-wasting behavior! Get on with it! Hup! Hup!*

It might be that a good kick in the pants from your drill-sergeant self can help you get going. Think you don't have an inner drill sergeant? You do. This strong voice *is* inside of you, even on your darkest days. You can talk to yourself this way and still be kind to yourself. You can say, *Get up! Get out of that bed! Get going! Don't listen to what's going on in your head. Put on some nice clothes! That's right, nice clothes, not those old sweats. You're going out. You're going to look like you care even if you don't!*

You need a drill sergeant when …

- Your depressed thoughts are so negative you find it hard to move.
- You want to hide in bed all day.
- You can't get started on anything.

- You feel hopeless and worthless.
- You think you have no control on how your day will turn out.

You have just as much vocal power as depression does. You just need to know when you need to use it.

Alex's Story

I work by myself and often feel that being alone with my depression is an impossible situation. I wish I had someone to just tell me what to do and how to do it! I know I could work for others, but in reality, I do better alone. When I'm not depressed, I'm happy about working alone. When I'm depressed, I need something to get me going. Often "me" is all I need because I can be two people. I can yell at myself when I'm feeling down. This is the "real me" talking to the "sick me." *You will work for six hours today, Alex! You will wash your face and get out that door! Get to it. Move!* My brain responds to this, for some reason. I certainly wouldn't like it from a real person, but I can take it from myself. It's like clearing a really messy path so I can walk through it. *Walk! March!*—this is the real me.

My Story

I cry a lot when I'm depressed. I sometimes wake up crying for no reason. It's terrible. I lie in bed wondering why I should even get up. I now know these are the days when I need to channel my inner drill sergeant. *Okay, Julie. Get up.* And I get out of bed. *Get going, Julie. Put on your clothes, choose some earrings, and look nice.* I don't want to do any of this because it truly seems absolutely pointless. *Come on, Julie! Enough! You're not going to let this depression ruin your day. You* will *get up and get out of the house! Move!* It works, even on the really bad days. It's like a routine now. That inner voice has to take over to get me moving. I'm not sure when I figured out to do this. I do know that for many years, I often didn't make it out of bed, but now I always do. Always.

What I do now:

- I conjure up the strong me to talk to the ill me.
- I'm not scared to yell at myself. Depression can make me really wimpy and passive, and I want to get out of that mood no matter what.
- I'm willing to try anything to get myself out of bed.

Exercise

Think of a person you respect. It can be someone you know, someone famous, someone from a movie, or someone from a book—it doesn't matter. Now write down what this person would say to you when it's hard for you to get out of bed. How about when it's time to choose clothes for the day or get the kids' lunches ready? What would the person say when you're staring into space at your desk? What if you have a social event to go to? Imagine a day when you have something due and just can't seem to get started. Then listen to the voice of your imaginary drill sergeant and get moving!

Here's an example using Scarlet O'Hara: *Today is a hard day, Julie. You're filled with worry and fear. You can't imagine how you'll move on. But you can and you will! Who are you? You're a woman, and you're strong!*

Fiddledeedee! Nothing will ever get you down. Not a burning city, not losing your husband, not making clothes out of curtains. Don't focus on tomorrow like I did. Focus on today. *Now get going, Julie! What's first? Do it now!*

Now you channel the voice of your inner drill sergeant and listen to what he or she says:

My person: _____

Their words: _____

_____

_____

_____

_____

ASK DR. PRESTON

Q **Why does talking to yourself in a tough way help you get started and keep going?**

A Being strong with yourself can help you find that burst of energy you need to get started on something. Once you get moving, it's best not to stop, or else it's easy to collapse back onto the couch. It's so important to maintain momentum.

If such inner coaching is done in a proactive and forceful way without being too harsh, it can be used to ward off or fight against the urge to just surrender or give up. Listening to that inner dialogue can be an antidote to the powerlessness depression often causes. And your own inner tough talk can be easier to hear because you know it's from a desire to get better; you know it's not criticism, as you could perceive it if it came from someone else.

Always Be Kind to Yourself

It's important to note that this drill sergeant voice is never negative. It doesn't help at all if you get on yourself for being worthless and a failure. Your inner drill sergeant can be loud, strong, aggressive, and practical, but he or she is never mean. You can see this persona as a friend who truly wants you to do well, a guide on the days depression won't really let you get on with your life.

Here are some other thoughts to consider:

- Physically control your own actions by encouraging yourself to get up and get going.

- When you get started, use your inner drill sergeant voice all day to keep you going.

- Let your drill sergeant—*not* your depression—do the thinking.

- Be willing to try anything to get better so you can get things done.

Remember: On the days when you need extra help to get out of bed or do anything productive, call up your inner drill sergeant. He or she exists to help you get things done, so listen up!

Structure Your Day Like a Child's

Have you ever noticed how depression makes you feel like you're floating through the day with no purpose? When your life feels out of control and without structure, it's natural to feel like you'll never get your depression under control. And then you have even more trouble getting things done. Like a child, you'll probably respond to chaos with more chaos in your mind.

Children are easily distracted by all that goes on around them. Having structured meal times, play times, television times, and bedtimes can create a calm and balanced child as opposed to the cranky and difficult child who flounders with little to no structure. Having the same kind of structure in place can work for you, too.

The Importance of Structure

For most of your childhood and adolescence, the structure of your daily life was probably decided for you. In high school, you were probably given a bit more leeway, but the structure was still pretty intense. Then when you were thrown out into the real world, whether in a job or at college, all the structure you were probably used to others establishing for you, especially your parents, simply went away. This transition can be hard for anyone, but when you add depression to the mix, the situation can get out of control. It's not surprising, then, that so many people can become depressed and overwhelmed on their first jobs or at a new school. As an adult who has depression, you may still struggle as much as someone fresh out of high school.

When you're depressed, it always helps to know in advance what your day will look like. One of the best ways to do this is to have a plan in place on all days so you know what to do when the depression shows up. You have enough to worry about when you're in a down mood; knowing what your day will look like removes one more pressure that can lead to less productivity.

Do you recognize in yourself any of the following signs indicating you need more structure?

- Waking up depressed because you have no plan for the day and nothing to look forward to.
- Drifting around looking for something to do.
- Randomly going from project to project.
- No idea what you're going to do for the next week.
- Assuming you can create a structure as you go. (This might work on well days, but it rarely works on depressed days.)

Even one planned event a day can make a difference. Knowing that you have to be at a certain place at a certain time makes it easier for you to get things done before and after the event.

Melissa's Story

I wish I lived in a commune or military barracks or in some setup where I'd be told what to do and when. Making those choices for myself doesn't work lately. I want a structure decided for me. I know it would help if I worked outside the home, but I don't. It's my choice to stay home with my kids, but when they're in school, I can literally walk around my house for hours. I pick up one thing and then turn on the TV and then call my husband and then watch more TV and then think of how I'm wasting my time … it just doesn't stop. I have plenty of friends to see, but their lives seem so much more structured than mine.

I've decided to make a change and apply for a part-time job. I thought staying home would be good for me, but it was the wrong decision. My kids will be fine if they have to go to day care a few hours in the afternoons. I think this is much better than having a depressed mother walking around the house for hours just waiting for them to get home.

My Story

One of my biggest problems with not being able to work in an office setting (where my depression gets worse due to stress) is that writing is the least structured of any career I can think of! But I so long for structure.

And I think life is more structured when you have others to take care of, but because I don't have children, I also don't have that structure. I'm now working on planning my days by taking classes and making sure I have something to do in the late afternoon, so I know I have to stop working at a specific time.

There are so many days when I feel like I'm floating. On these days, I get nothing done. The night is rarely a problem for me because that's when I see the people who work during the day, but the daytime can be a huge problem if it's unstructured.

What I do now:

- I know I have to make plans far in advance.

- I need something to look forward to because I really flounder if I wake up depressed and without a plan.

- I remind people that I need a lot of structure and it really helps if they stick to our previously decided times and plans. This used to seem a bit controlling to my family and friends, but I think they really understand now and try hard to accommodate me.

- When I look at my day planner and it's empty, I know I have to schedule work and events very specifically.

- On the days when I have too much free time, I go easy on myself if I get really upset and more depressed. And then I make sure I have something to do the next day.

Exercise

What was your school day like in the sixth grade? It might take a while to remember, but you can probably plot out the whole year with just a few sentences:

_____

_____

_____

Compare this to your day today:

_____

_____

_____

How can you create a similar structure?

_____

_____

_____

If you already have a very structured day, is it helpful to you? If not, what do you need to change?

_____

_____

_____

ASK DR. PRESTON

Q **Why does depression often respond to structure?**

A To answer this question, let's look at someone who has a free Saturday ahead of them. If there's no structure, no planned activities, the depressed person is at high risk for staying in bed or otherwise not engaging in any enjoyable or meaningful activity. Often, by the end of the day, they've accomplished nothing and think, *I got nothing done. I didn't see anyone. I feel useless and lonely. I feel out of control of my life.* In addition, inactivity leads to lethargy and fatigue.

But when you have a plan, a structure, in place, you have something to look forward to, and that helps lift the depression.

You Need Structure!

Children respond to structure. Let them run wild all day, and you're asking for discipline and sleep problems. It's the same with your brain. Structure creates calmness. Knowing you have to be somewhere or do something at a certain time helps you get things done. Without structure in place, you can lose days, weeks, months, and even years floating around wondering why you can't get anything done. Structure your life, and structure your brain.

Here are some more benefits of structure:

- You're more able to focus on what needs to be done instead of when it'll be done.

- Having things the same on a daily basis may be a bit boring or seem too busy on the good days, but it helps immensely on depressed days.

- Decide what you'll do in advance so you don't have to make what seem like impossible decisions on your depressed days.

- It can be a huge relief to know that you have something planned and something to look forward to.

Remember: Not having a plan for your depressed days can lead to more depression; this is simply because you have more time to think about what's wrong with your life instead of getting out there and living it. Begin to put a structure in place now. Don't wait.

8

Remind Yourself That You're Depressed

Have you ever had a day when you stand up and you're ready to do something ... but by the time you make the first move on the project you just feel like all your energy is gone and you have to sit down again? Are there some days when you just can't see why it's so hard to do things? Do you think, *Other people do these things with no problems. Why is it so hard for me?*

It's hard for you because you have an illness that often makes it *impossible* to get things done with ease. It's so easy to forget how depression affects your life; it's as though you have amnesia. You can have days on which things are difficult and then you get better and get on with your life. When the difficult days come back, you think, *What's wrong with me? I was doing just fine!* This lack of awareness is very common for people with depression. If you had physical signs such as a high fever, it would be easy to know what was happening. But depression is so silent. It can sneak up on you and catch you unaware.

Dealing with Catatonic Depression

Catatonic depression is the type of depression where even brushing your teeth seems impossible. You get up in the morning, and before you know it, you're sitting in a chair staring out the window and you can't get up. Your brain feels blank and overwhelmingly depressed at the same time. You may stand for long periods or have trouble making the choice where to walk. This depression is particularly hard to fight.

On these days, it's especially important for you to remind yourself that it's depression causing these problems and that you can still move. You can lift your hands, and you can walk. You can do what you need to do. You're depressed but not truly frozen. Reminding yourself that you're depressed helps you focus on what the illness is doing to you instead of what you're doing wrong.

Be aware of these signs to help remind yourself that you're depressed:

- You attribute your problems getting things done to a lack of motivation.

- When others tell you that you should do more, you agree but find it hard to follow through.

- You're ashamed that the day is so hard and you often cry about it.

- You feel confused as to why things are so incredibly difficult.

When you learn your own depression signs, you can stop and remind yourself that it's depression before you lose another day to self-criticism.

Matt's Story

Here's how I used to think: *You're stupid and worthless, Matt. Other people at the office get things done. You're going to get fired. Everyone can see that your work sucks. Look at how you're dressed—you don't even look professional. You met with that PR woman the other day, and there's no way she's going to collaborate with you. You're too fat and your jacket is too small.* It was terrible.

Then I realized that I don't think this way when I'm not depressed. I started to talk back to myself. I said, *I'm depressed,* whenever any of these thoughts came up. I told myself, *Depression is an illness, and I have depression. These thoughts happen because I have depression. I can get things done even when depression can't.* Sometimes it's really difficult to see what's going on and I can focus on my imaginary failings for hours; but I've taught myself what I say to myself when I'm depressed and I'm more ready for it now.

My Story

When I have a project due and the depression is really tough, I coach myself through the day. *Okay, Julie. You're depressed. This is normal. Just sit down at the computer and do part of the work.* When I manage to do part of the work—and I can do more now than I ever used to be able to do—I often start staring into space again. So I start over. *Julie, this is normal. You're depressed. Try again. You can do it, Julie. Depression makes you like this. You can work!* I know it's like talking to a child, but it gets the job done on days my brain is barely functioning.

Here's what I say to myself when I'm just sitting or lying in bed in a stupor:

- *I'm lying here because I'm depressed. I will get up.*

- *I won't let this depression take over my actions. It may have taken over my mind, but not my actions.*

- *This is depression. It's not the real me. Where is the real me, and what would she do?*

- *I don't have to want to get up and break this catatonic feeling, but I will make myself move. I will get up. My own voice and thoughts are stronger than depression.*

Exercise

A depressed brain can feel like a dead brain. Saying something once might not be enough; on the really tough days, you may need to repeat something over and over just to get yourself through the day. This is why you can use a *mantra*—a word or formula chanted or sung as an incantation or prayer—to keep yourself moving.

For example, here's what I could use: *It's okay, Julie. You can do it. It's just depression. Just do what you can. Nothing is wrong, Julie. Nothing has changed.* I will sit in a chair and feel like I can't get up, and I'll say it again. *It's okay, Julie. You can do it. It's just depression. Just do what you can. Nothing is wrong, Julie. Nothing has changed.* Saying "nothing has changed" is a very important part of my mantra. It keeps me from looking for something wrong in my life when the only thing that is really wrong is that I'm depressed.

Write your mantra here:

_____

_____

_____

_____

_____

_____

_____

It helps if you memorize this mantra. It can be a form of meditation or something you say out loud. Be sure you use your name in the mantra and say it all day long!

Ask Dr. Preston

Q **Why does it help depressed people to remind themselves that they're depressed?**

A It's important to be ever-aware that depression is influencing most if not all of your perceptions and conclusions. You always need to be on the alert to carefully evaluate what you're thinking. Also, when you're depressed, you need to be watchful for harsh and negative self-talk. Reminding yourself that you're depressed keeps you from being overly critical; during this time especially, you need to be gentle and compassionate toward yourself.

Talk to Yourself All Day

It's okay to talk to yourself all the time when you're depressed. This overrides what your depressed brain might say, and it reminds you that it's an illness and not you. It's so easy to forget this when you're in the middle of a day when your productivity is very low, so work on reminding yourself that you're depressed until it becomes your mantra.

Here are some other thoughts to consider:

- Become an observer of your own depression. When you see it taking over, use your mantra to remind yourself that there's nothing wrong with you or your life—you're simply depressed.

- If you're the visual type, put a copy of your mantra in your purse or wallet. If you're musical, sing the mantra. Do whatever it takes for you.

- Use repetition to get through to your depressed brain. It works.

Remember: On the days when you can't seem to get anything done and everything seems to go wrong, remind yourself that you're depressed. Tell yourself feeling this way is normal and keep going.

Eliminate Distractions

Lack of focus and a feeling of confusion are very normal when you're depressed and can make you very easily distracted. That, in turn, can lead to a lot of problems when you have to get something done, especially on a deadline. Working alone at home, for example, might feel impossible, so you get up and turn on the TV, call a friend, or do anything except what you need to do.

If you're depressed, it's natural that you would want to do something that seems more pleasurable than a required task. And a distracted brain often needs a fix before it can calm down.

Making Deals with Yourself

If you want to feel better when you feel scattered and unfocused, you might even negotiate this: *I'm just going to make one phone call and then I'll feel better* ... and suddenly it's an hour of phone calls because they calm you down.

You've given your distracted brain something to do, but the problem is that it's not what you needed to do! It's hard to understand why it would be easier to do something you don't need to do than actually just do what you have to do, but depression is confusing like that. You can have plenty of energy to do what doesn't need to be done right now but feel absolutely worn out when faced with a required task.

When something suddenly seems far more appealing than your actual project, don't give in to the distraction. Be sure you work productively on the unfocused days. You can do this by putting yourself in a place with few to no distractions. Or you can remove as many distractions as possible before you even start to work.

Are any of the following common distractions for you?

- E-mail/Internet/phone
- Television
- Rearranging your desk
- Walking through the halls talking with colleagues

- Suddenly needing to find something (and getting up to look)
- Family members

It's so easy to become distracted today. Take the time to look around you and see what pulls your attention away from your task. This helps you know where you need to make changes.

Justin's Story

I know the Internet and e-mail are amazing inventions, but in terms of working when I can't focus, they have been a terrible addition to my life! I have the Internet at work, and I'm usually okay with it. But it becomes *so* incredibly enticing when I'm having a low day.

And why does e-mail suddenly become so important? I can exchange e-mail after e-mail with my friends on these days instead of working. And then I feel rotten and stupid and even more depressed at the end of the day. These are friends I can call anytime when I get home—where I also have the Internet.

I have a lot of questions about what my brain is doing when this happens. Is it misfiring? Does the distraction make me feel better? It does sometimes, as I feel a moment of relief, but then I'm right back there needing more. I think this has to do with the fact that I have ADHD (attention-deficit hyperactivity disorder) and OCD (obsessive-compulsive disorder) symptoms when I get depressed.

Now I have a rule: when the behavior gets out of hand—and I usually don't notice it until I've wasted a few hours—I leave my office and work in a conference room. Now that we have wireless, it's hard to stay away from the Internet or e-mail, but moving myself into a place with fewer distractions works.

My Story

I always want to clean my house when I have a writing deadline. Especially my kitchen floor. Believe me, cleaning my house is not usually that compelling, but it always comes up when a chapter is due. I then think of organizing all the pictures I've had sitting in a box for the past few years. Or how it would be great to finally organize my e-mail! And make a shopping list ... and organize my clothes ... and all the other things I dread doing when I have the time.

I now know that wanting to distract myself means I need to get back to the project. I also know that distractions feel good when

I'm depressed because they get me out of the routine. But in reality, they disrupt the routine and I get even more behind than usual.

What I do now:

- Work at a college library where I don't have access to the Internet.
- Turn off my cell phone.
- Do noncomputer work, such as hardcopy editing, at a coffee shop.
- Negotiate with myself in a good way: *When you finish a chapter, Julie, you can go get some coffee.* (Decaf, of course!)
- Enjoy the clean house I always have when I finish editing a book!

Exercise

What are your main distractions? The following table lists some; are they in your control or out of your control? Some distractions may only sometimes be in your control. If this is so, check both boxes.

Distraction	In My Control	Out of My Control
Cell phone	☐	☐
E-mail	☐	☐
Internet	☐	☐
Children	☐	☐
Co-workers	☐	☐
Meetings	☐	☐
Loud noises	☐	☐
Uncomfortable work space	☐	☐
Television	☐	☐
Other:		
_____	☐	☐
_____	☐	☐
_____	☐	☐

Look over these distractions and decide what you can do about them. For example, you can turn off the TV and make a rule that you don't watch TV on your depressed days. Think of all the distractions you can remove now and make tomorrow a more productive day.

ASK DR. PRESTON

Q **Why is a depressed brain so easily distracted?**

A The human brain's frontal lobes perform a number of important tasks, including helping you maintain concentration and attention. Due to changes in the brain when you're depressed, the frontal lobes can fail to help you keep your attention adequately focused. That might make it difficult for you to pay attention and may also cause you to become easily distracted.

And when you're suffering from serious depression, your inner thoughts can be dominated by constant worries. You become so preoccupied with negative self-talk that it detracts from your ability to stay tuned in to what's happening moment to moment. So when you're presented with something that offers more positive feelings, your brain tells you to go for it.

Focus on Your Work

When you're depressed, it's easier to focus on anything *but* what you have to do. The more distractions you get out of the way and the more you remind yourself that you need to work, not play with gadgets or call your friends, the better chance you have of completing what you have to do.

Here are some other thoughts to consider:

- Recognize that wanting to do the things you normally couldn't care less about is a sign that you're getting distracted and that you need to stop now!

- Get rid of your television or stop watching it when you're depressed.

- Turn off your cell phone when you're working, or make a pact with yourself to only answer professional calls. Or leave your cell phone in the car or at home when you're at work. People survived just fine without cell phones for a very long time; a few hours away from yours during your depressed days isn't going to hurt.

- Go to a space that doesn't have the Internet or any other distractions you may have trouble with.

Remember: When you remove distractions and get work done, you'll feel a lot better than if you spent all day on worthless pursuits.

10

Think Like an Athlete

On many days, it's a probability that athletes just don't want to train or compete. They might not feel their best, they might be having personal problems, or they might be struggling with a coach or a teammate. And yet great athletes find a way to get past all that. One of their main skills is the ability to separate physical activity from negative mental thoughts.

You may be faced with the same situations an athlete faces when they must train and compete no matter how they feel. This is especially true if you have a physical task you need to complete. But take heart: you can use the tools athletes use to finish your project, even when your mind is screaming that it's impossible. The mind and body work as a unit, but when the brain isn't functioning the way it should, making a mind-body split can be a good thing.

Just Do It … Anyway

"Just do it!" How many times have you heard Nike's popular slogan bandied about by a good-intentioned friend or co-worker when you feel that you just don't have the skills or energy to do something physical? People with depression face this situation all the time. When you're depressed, hearing "Just do it" may seem ridiculous. If you could just do it, you would!

But you *can* do it. You just have to turn off your mind and turn on your body. You might not feel like you have the ability to do what needs to be done, but you can't know this until you try. This is why you need to just do it … anyway.

Beware of these barriers to completing physical tasks:

- You feel lethargic.
- You want to quit.
- Your depressed thoughts control your physical actions.
- You feel unable to get up, much less do something strenuous.

On the really tough days, close your eyes and picture what your favorite athlete would do. This can help you focus on the task instead of staying in bed all day!

Peter's Story

I play minor league baseball for a living and find that I get especially depressed on the road. I don't have a real support system and often feel the urge to just quit and go home, but I know that would depress me even more than staying on the team. I hide my depression a lot, but I've told a few people. My coach, who I've told, has similar problems. He was honest with me, and it really helped.

I don't know how I do it, but I really am able to get on the field and play no matter how I'm feeling. I can feel down before a game and think there's no way I can play. But when I'm on the field, I focus on the ball and the sounds and the happiness I feel to be doing something I love. Sometimes the depression is back as soon as I'm back on the bus, but I live for the physical stuff. I know I'm a lot less depressed when I'm active.

My Story

I can think of many instances when I have to do something physical even when my brain is not at its best. I used to let this get in the way of exercise. It all just seemed so overwhelming. It was the same with cleaning the house—I once let my yard grow until it looked like a wheat field. If a professional football player acted this way, he would be out of a job pretty quickly.

I always ask myself, *How do these guys do this? How does a tennis player go to Wimbledon and play even when she's not at her best mentally? How does a baseball player play so many games in a season without taking a break? He must have some kind of magic potion!* I think it's their ability to just do the physical and keep all mental thoughts on the physical game. They have to push aside doubt, pain, and fear and just keep going. I try to do this when I'm faced with a physical task I have to get done. It's better than having a lawn that looks like a wheat field!

What I do now:

- I remember that I have control over my physical action. The impulse from my brain to my hand might be messed up when I'm depressed, but my actual physical body is fine.

- I constantly remind myself that I always feel better when I do something physical. *Always.*

- Doing something physical usually involves being around other people. This helps me feel less isolated, too.

Exercise

Ask yourself the following questions:

What are the five characteristics of successful athletes?

_____

_____

_____

_____

_____

What athlete do you particularly admire? Why do you admire this person?

_____

_____

_____

_____

How can you apply this athletic ability and work ethic to your life even when you're depressed?

_____

_____

_____

_____

_____

ASK DR. PRESTON

Q **Why are athletes able to continue to do their jobs even if they get depressed?**

A The tasks an athlete undertakes for athletic events are pretty clearly defined. And the more a depressed person has concrete plans, the easier it is for him or her to know what to do. So many problems facing depressed people are vague, abstract, or very complex (for example, *How do I improve the quality of my marriage* or *What can I do to deal with my grief over the loss of a loved one?*). The Nike slogan "Just do it" is more defined for athletes. So when people are depressed, the more they can define their tasks and think like an athlete, the more manageable their tasks seem.

Athletes Get It Done!

Professional athletes rarely miss games; they perform because they have to. You can do the same. Set rules for yourself. If you have to be somewhere at a certain time, go no matter how you feel. If you have a job that requires physical stamina, remind yourself that you will find the energy once you're on the job. As harsh as this sounds, depression is not a reason to miss a physical activity. You are your own coach. Be hard on yourself if appropriate, and show up when you have to.

On the days when you feel like a motionless blob, think of the following:

Work with a team. Physical projects often go better when you have a teammate. If your yard needs cleaning, you have to move, or you need to change the breaks on your car, ask for help. Even if someone is there just to hand you a tool and talk with you, that company can help you stay focused on the physical task. It can also take your mind off your depression.

Visualize exercise success. Exercise is one of the best ways to deal with depression, yet you can feel so completely against doing the exercise that it often feels better to just sit around and stay depressed. The next time you feel this way, imagine you're training for a big event and then visualize your success. Maybe it's a 10K run or a softball game. You may even see yourself winning a gold medal at the Olympics. You can decide what works for you. Visualization may feel silly at first, but it's a proven technique, and many successful athletes do it regularly.

Deal with the mental after you're done with the physical. It's a good idea to focus your energy on the project at hand instead of stopping to listen to what your brain is saying. When negative thoughts come up, say to yourself, *I will finish this project and then I will think about the depression.* Physical activity can give you a break from the constant chatter depression can cause. (What a relief!) You may also find that the physical activity helps the depression and that the project was not nearly as bad as you thought it would be.

Focus on the goal, not the individual work. If you stress over all the small steps a project will take, it can very likely keep you from getting started at all. Thinking about a project like that would be like breaking a workout session into each individual repetition. No one wants to think of how many sit-ups, stair-climber steps, and leg lifts they'll have to do to complete one hour of exercise. It's easier and more effective to focus on your overall goal. Feeling better physically, sitting in a new apartment with all your stuff around you, or driving a clean car focuses on what you accomplish instead of how hard it was to get there.

Remember: Athletes have to get things done no matter how they feel. They perform with broken bones, aching backs, and lack of sleep. And considering the number of people with depression in the United States, there's a good chance that quite a few athletes get things done when they're depressed. You can do it, too.

11

Expect Brain Chatter

Depression can often create a running commentary in your brain when you try to get something done—it's like being followed by a nasty critic who won't shut up! Sometimes the chatter is so effective you may stop a project just to get it to shut up.

It can feel very uncomfortable and stressful to actually hear your thoughts in a rapid fashion. This brain chatter can often make you feel as if there's an auctioneer in your head. It's distracting and sometimes even scary.

The Chatter Is Normal

Physical depression takes two main forms: lethargy and agitation. (The thoughts of worthlessness and hopelessness are the same with both types; the delivery of the thoughts is simply different.) With lethargic depression, the brain slows down almost to a stop, and the person feels constantly tired and worn out. Agitated depression is the opposite. Sleep is very difficult and strong anxiety is the norm.

Brain chatter is an almost constant companion if you have agitated depression. The chatter can cause severe sleep deprivation, which naturally leads to productivity problems. In addition, and perhaps worse, brain chatter won't leave you alone, and dealing with the chatter sucks up a lot of your energy that could go toward work and other obligations.

If you have agitated depression, excessive brain chatter can also be a clue that you're doing too much, you're overwhelmed, your medications are not working correctly, you've taken an overstimulating herb, or you've had too much caffeine or not enough sleep. It helps to look into these areas as soon as the chatter starts. The key is to recognize the chatter, take care of it in the moment, and then see what triggered it so you can prevent it in the future.

Here are some tips for recognizing brain chatter:

- It's often repetitive, fast, and very difficult to follow.
- It focuses on one project and doesn't stop until you either finish or quit the project.

- It can feel like a broken record—you can actually hear parts of songs or parts of conversations you had earlier loop over and over for hours.

- It's usually negative and very oriented toward worry.

- It's distracting and often makes work difficult.

- The chatter can significantly affect your sleep.

When you're aware of what this chatter sounds like to you, you can at least know that it's caused by depression and that you can get things done even when it's raging.

Patty's Story

Here's a sample of what my brain chatter said at work the other day: *This is not the desk for you. You need to clean this desk. It's noisy here. You need to shut your door. What work are you doing? You're behind on this work. Get up and do something. What are you having for lunch? What is your problem?* I actually wrote this down as I was hearing it. There's no way I could have remembered it otherwise.

My brain chatter is like mental gymnastics. It tires me. I wish I could say there's always an easy solution to get it to stop, but I have difficulty with it. When I'm depressed, it's hard enough to deal with the slow thoughts, but these racing thoughts attack me so quickly I want to put my head in my hands and squeeze them out! I know getting enough sleep helps, as does keeping the noise around me at a minimum to prevent my brain from picking up sounds and repeating them over and over.

My Story

Brain chatter is one of my main problems with depression. I definitely have lethargic and agitated depression, and I hate both of them, but this brain-in-a-blender stuff is really terrible. There are days when I actually feel my thoughts are following me around. They talk to me and try to get me to quit a project because they tell me I won't do a good job.

I also get the chatter that tells me I need to do something else to be happy. This chatter is different from the other depressive thoughts I have because it's so frantic. It's a barrage that doesn't stop. I can't even sit and count how many thoughts there are, they come so fast. I'll hear the same thought over and over again: *You'll always be alone. You'll always be alone. You'll always be alone.* And then when I'm not alone, the chatter switches to something else: *You'll never sell another book. You'll never sell another book. You'll never sell another book.* Thanks, brain! And that's not all—a thousand other thoughts and sounds go on at the same time. These are just the main thoughts.

What I do now:

- I'm really, really careful not to stay out too late, even if I'm having a great time at karaoke.

- I limit alcohol and caffeinated coffee because they really mess up my sleep. My brain runs all night if I don't watch it.

- I make myself sleep enough. I often have to take sleep medications.

- I take medications for anxiety when I get desperate.

- As much as I can, I keep away from stressful people and situations.

Is my life less fun because of a few of these things? Probably. But it's a trade-off.

Exercise

Listen to the song "Revolution #9" by The Beatles. This song somehow captures the brain chatter of depression. If rumors are true, this song was created with more than a little help from mind-altering substances, but it's an interesting experience to hear an external recording of what usually goes on in your head. If someone asks you what it's like when your brain won't turn off, you can play this song as an example.

ASK DR. PRESTON

Q **What in the brain causes excessive brain chatter—the kind that's very distressing and sounds like a mean auctioneer?**

A Many people with depression are in an almost constant state of inner self-talk. They often go over and over what they've done wrong or what bad things might happen. They dwell on negative thoughts in ways that are nonproductive and just serve to stir up internal distress. This kind of rumination is somewhat similar to what happens in obsessive-compulsive disorder (OCD).

In your brain, there's a pathway between the frontal lobes that's an alarm circuit. This gets activated when your brain senses potential trouble or danger, and the neural pathways become engaged, promoting increased attention and vigilance.

It's also important to note that 50 percent of people with depression have agitated depression or depression that's accompanied by significant anxiety. Such people are more prone to have lots of negative self-talk and hear the chatter. The other half are more lethargic and slow in their thinking and behavior.

The Brain Chatter Merry-Go-Round

Brain chatter can often make you feel like you're on a merry-go-round that will never stop. You want to get off, but it feels impossible. When this happens, remind yourself that this is normal, and work on calming down your mind instead of worrying about all the negative thoughts going through your head. Brain chatter is one of the symptoms of depression you can control through life management.

Brain chatter can severely limit your ability to focus on a task, so the more you can reduce the chatter, the easier it will be to get things done.

Here are some other thoughts to consider:

- Break brain chatter by filling your mind with other thoughts by doing something that requires you to use your brain.
- Say "NO!" or "STOP!" out loud.
- Get help for anxiety.
- Sleep! A tired mind is often a chatty mind. If the brain chatter keeps you awake, talk with your doctor about sleep management.
- Watch the caffeine and alcohol. Both can cause the chatter, and both definitely can cause sleep problems that lead to more chatter.
- Explore meditation options. It may be that a practice that replaces the brain chatter with specific chants or music can help significantly.

Remember: Brain chatter can be a sign of anxiety, sleep problems, or that you're doing too much. Ask yourself, *Is there anything I've done or has anything happened to cause my brain to get so out of control?*

Write Yourself a Letter

A depressed brain is an unreasonable brain. People you care about can tell you, "You're so talented! You definitely have the ability to do your work." But your depressed brain might overlook the compliment and only hear, "You just need to sit down and get going!" And with that kind of thinking, the advice and support people offer can seem endless and often frustrating.

For most depressed people, it's hard to believe what other people say. The ability to reasonably think, *Hey! They're right!* is completely absent.

Depression Makes You Blind to Others' Help

When you're depressed, the well wishes and help others offer can feel very annoying. You think, *If they just lived a day in my shoes, they wouldn't be telling me how easy it is to just do something with my life!* As a result, you may tune out all the advice and keep going in your misery. This blind, pessimistic thinking can make your depression much worse and even further isolate you from the people who want to help.

One of the most effective ways to counteract this blindness is to recognize that the "well you" might be the best person to listen to when you need help. But how do you get through to yourself when you're depressed and don't want to listen? You have to look inside yourself so the well you can write positive messages the depressed you can read later.

You need to help yourself when …

- Help from others feels useless.
- You're sure nothing will help.
- You're unable to see how you can help yourself.
- You resist the idea because you're not big on affirmations or any "New Age-y" stuff!
- You realize you've been under the spell of depression for too long and it's time for you to take control.

Using yourself as a tool to get things done may feel odd when you're depressed, but the well you *is* inside there, and you need to utilize this part of you all you can!

Carlos's Story

I've created affirmations and placed them all over my house. My refrigerator holds this one: *You can break the depression cycle. It's up to you. You can make things different. It's up to you. You can do what is right for you, not what your brain is telling you to do. You can break the depression cycle, Carlos. Soon the uncomfortable depression feelings will pass. It's up to you.*

I have to move this sign around as I get used to it and forget to read it. It really is up to me to do what I can when I get sick. No one else is there to take care of me.

My Story

When I look back over my 20 years of untreated depression, I can't think of many times when I said nice things about myself. I let the depression think for me. When I was well, I was pretty normal. But the depressed me was a monster who hated the real me. I find it hard to even come up with the language depression used to say to me. It was all I listened to. I never saw anything positive in what I did. I ran away from things a lot to try to find something that made me feel better about my work. I never found it.

What I do now:

- I write notes like this to myself in my journal all the time:

    Tonight is a good night, Julie! Don't forget that you have them. The book is going well. The ideas are flowing. It came together really well this weekend. You're almost done with each strategy. Don't forget this, Julie. Tonight is a good night, and there will be other good nights.

- I try to remember to read the notes I write to myself. Serious depression makes me forget to look at them.

- Reading notes to myself helps put me in touch with the real me. This keeps me from giving in to what the depressed me is saying.

Exercise

Use the following example to write a note to yourself that you can read when you feel ill, hopeless, or unproductive:

Hello *(your name here)*,

I want to remind you what you're like when you're not depressed. You get things done with ease. In fact, you don't even have to think of most things such as cooking dinner or reading to your nephew. You go to work, sit down, and do what you have to do. When you get up in the morning you either just get going or you have the thought that the day is going to be a good day. You don't think about the past, and you certainly don't have negative thoughts all day that tell you what you're doing wrong. You work like a normal person and feel a sense of accomplishment. You're able to have fun and look forward to your evening when you can relax. You don't have trouble getting to sleep. And you wake up the next day with pleasure and anticipation for what will happen that day.

Remember this,
Your well self

Now, write your own letter:

_____

_____

_____

_____

_____

_____

_____

Put your letter in your desk or on the wall. Or give it to a family member or friend and ask them to give you the letter when they see that you're having trouble due to depression. This lets them get involved when you're not able to ask for help in the moment.

ASK DR. PRESTON

Q **Why can a depressed person listen to advice they wrote down when well, yet have trouble listening to advice from others?**

A When people are struggling with depression, they almost always get bombarded with "good advice." The words are often sincere, but not so helpful: *Snap out of it! Try harder! You'll get over it! Look on the bright side! It can't be all that bad!* This leaves the depressed person feeling misunderstood. They believe that others can't really know how they're feeling, which can be entirely true.

But the depressed person knows their well self knows how they're feeling. They know that what comes from their well self is more likely to helpful.

The Advice from the Well You Is the Best Advice

Encouragement and a reality check from the well you in your own words is much more helpful than a well-meaning but unrealistic outside voice offering the same support. A note you've written to yourself when you're well and on a day when you were able to work normally can help remind you that depression is often the cause of your productivity problems, not a failing in yourself.

Here are some other thoughts to consider:

- Work hard to overcome the feeling that this—writing a letter to yourself—is a silly idea you don't think will work.

- Write this letter only when you're well. That's when you're the most reasonable.

- If it's still too hard to write, ask someone who knows you well to write a letter to you about how you are when you're not depressed.

Remember: We often listen to ourselves more than we listen to others. Let your well self communicate with your ill self through a letter. It's like a message in a bottle you find when you really feel isolated. It could be just the message you need on a tough day.

13

Break Through the Depression Barrier

Some days, depression can feel like a heavy barrier over your head that's so oppressive it's hard to function. Not only can this be very frustrating, it can also be downright scary. It's hard enough to deal with the negative thoughts caused by depression without having to deal with this physical feeling as well.

Think of how your body feels when you're depressed. There's a good chance that along with the negative thoughts, you also feel a sense of oppression as though you're surrounded by an unseen force that's zapping your energy and making it difficult for you to function the way you'd like.

You Can Break Through

When you feel so physically helpless, acknowledge it as a sign that you're being confined by depression. Recognizing the feeling before it literally keeps you from moving is a positive step in learning more about how depression can affect and limit your life. Just as some workers feel they are held back by a glass ceiling, when you're depressed, you might feel a dark ceiling over your head that you can't break through to get things done the way you want to.

These are the days when you have to think like a superhero and imagine yourself breaking through the barrier in order to move forward with the strategies in this book. When you do manage to lift the physically oppressed feeling, it can be as though the world goes from dark to light and your entire body feels like it has been set free.

Are you being squashed by the depression barrier?

- Does your body feel uncomfortable and squeezed?
- Do you feel like you're in a box of misery?
- Do colors around you feel dark?
- Are you isolated in your own mind?
- Do you feel physically limited?

The depression barrier may be one of the first things you notice when you're depressed. Use this recognition as a motivation for expanding your body and saying no to the feeling of physical limitation.

Robin's Story

When I am particularly depressed, I feel like I'm enclosed in a black box. I sometimes feel this way mentally, as though there's a dark fog around me, but the box feeling is like something is physically encircling me and making me miserable. It prevents me from functioning the way I want to.

These are the days when I'm particularly depressed, but I do know that I can deal with this box! I usually wake up with the feeling and have a plan ready. I say to myself, *This is not real. I'm not being pressured or oppressed. My brain is having some kind of odd physical feeling reaction, but there's nothing really there.* I have a saying at my desk: *Work anyway, Robin. Work anyway.* I then move my body and stretch it as big as I can to remind me that I control my physical space.

I have no idea what's going on in my brain when this happens or why my body reacts this way, but I know this is one part of depression I can often physically work out of my body so I feel better in the evening.

My Story

I have days when it feels like something large and black is hanging over my head. It feels real, and it feels like it won't ever leave. It's so oppressive I sometimes can't even function. On the really bad days, I can feel it above me, trying to push down on my shoulders. It gets that bad. I look over my shoulder to get it to stop, but of course nothing's there. I know it's a physical symptom of depression and that there's nothing really wrong with me, but it's still a very troublesome part of my depression.

I often wonder, *How am I supposed to sit at my computer and write when I feel so overwhelmed physically?* I often get so mad and frustrated that I refuse to help myself. It's as though this "thing" prevents me from taking care of myself. When I try to work with this feeling, I often feel like I want to punch something just to break through it. I'd like to fight it out, but there's nothing to fight.

What I do now:

- I know what it feels like, so I can recognize it instead of always wondering, *Why do I feel so oppressed? Is there something physically wrong with me?*

- I see looking over my shoulder as a sign that I'm depressed and need to go easy on myself.

- I accept it and ignore it when I have to.

Exercise

When you're depressed, it's easy to feel your space getting smaller and smaller. But look around you right now. See how wide the room or your office or wherever you are really is. The world is wide, and you're a part of it. Picture the world from space. You are on the world, and you have plenty of room to expand. So expand! By literally making yourself bigger, you can create a feeling of well-being that helps you move on with your daily projects. Now look up and think of your head and the clear space over it. Then look all the way down your body, down to your feet. Your body is the same as it is when you're well.

ASK DR. PRESTON

Q **Why does everything feel so dark and oppressive when I'm depressed?**

A Because of changes in the brain during depression, depressed people have a very strong tendency to see negative life events in the world, in the past, in the future, and in themselves. These negatives are accentuated and can be very uncomfortable mentally and physically, to the point that the positive or beautiful are completely tuned out.

There's also a lack of vibrancy in perception, and many people who are very depressed don't register colors as keenly. The world looks like shades of gray. This can lead to an oppressive feeling that can often be felt physically as well.

The Oppressive Feeling Is Not Real

Although the depression barrier feels very strong and real, it's not. If you look up, you'll see there's nothing there. You're not in a box, and you can get things done even when you can't get rid of the feeling. Simply reminding yourself of this can help lift the pressure and help you be more physically comfortable throughout the day.

Here are some other thoughts to consider:

- Run or work out really hard.

- Visualize the oppression lifting from your body.

- Ignore it and move on with your day.

- Eat something really spicy. This can create endorphins that can help lift the physical feeling.

- Pump your fist in the air to remind yourself that you're in control of your space.

- Listen to the Gipsy Kings (or whatever gets you moving) and dance!

Remember: Feeling a physical presence over your head when you're depressed is uncomfortable, but it's normal, and most importantly, you can make it go away.

Feel the Depression ... and Do It Anyway

It's natural that you want to work on getting rid of your depression. That's often the main focus of your days when you're sick. You know you have to get better, and you don't want to be depressed for the rest of your life. Unfortunately, whatever you're currently doing to get better might not be progressing the way you want it to. And while you're working on this plan, you still have to get on with your work. That means you have to feel the depression ... and do it anyway. You might just have to let the depression sit there instead of fighting it.

Waking Up Depressed

Waking up gloomy, guilty, sad, irritated, or uneasy in general is a tough way to start the day. It's easy to give in to those feelings the minute you get out of bed. And there's a chance that the depression will stay with you all day.

But believe it or not, you don't have to waste these days, even the really tough ones. After all, if you only get in a few hours of work, that's better than nothing. When you're depressed, you're in a fog but you can still drive. You may be crying, but you can still fix dinner or go have coffee with a friend. When you get things done despite the depression, you can feel a real sense of accomplishment.

Are you experiencing any of these normal signs of depression?

- Depression makes you feel like you're carrying a heavy weight.
- Depression follows you around and talks to you.
- Depression takes away your pleasure and makes you cry.
- Depression makes you feel hopeless, gloomy, and sad.
- Depression makes you doubt everything you do.

The list is endless. But the reality is that you can feel all these things and still do what you have to do anyway. You can feel so sick you don't think you can get out of the bed, but you can. Working when you're depressed is harder and sadder than working when you're well, but it's important that you focus on the outcome and how you want to feel when you get to bed. When you can acknowledge to yourself, *I did what I could today despite feeling so sick,* you take control—perhaps more control than you thought possible.

Ellen's Story

Getting things done has many levels. It's not always about work. Because I have depression, sometimes that simply means a day is going to be hard—sometimes impossibly hard. I just deal with it all—the thoughts, the feeling of heavy doom, the sadness. All of it gets in the way of my productivity, and it would do this forever if I let it. My depression is chronic, and unless a miracle happens (that would be nice!), I will deal with it for all my life.

On many, many days I'm depressed all day. And it's definitely true that some days I don't and can't get things done. But these days are fewer now. I have taught myself that I can do the work anyway, no matter how depressed I am. And if I do have a day when it's truly impossible to get things done, I remind myself, *Ellen, it's an illness. It can be better tomorrow.* I'm a teacher, and when I need it, I try to get as much energy from my students as I can.

My Story

I wrote all my books—*all of them,* including this one—while I was battling depression; sometimes when I was seriously depressed and even suicidal. I had to. What were my options? Twenty more years of not really getting anything done? Twenty more years of starting a project and quitting before I was even halfway through? I'd had enough of that.

I no longer let depression be the reason I don't get things done. Some days are certainly tougher than others, but I can honestly say that in the past few years I've managed to stay out of bed during the day. (As small as that sounds, for those of us who spent what seems like years lying in bed, this is a big accomplishment!) I've gotten so good at this technique that people often say, "But you don't seem depressed at all!" I consider this my greatest achievement. My depression is the same as always, but what I get done is 100 percent better.

What I do now:

- I still have days when nothing gets done. But I also know that these days make me feel terrible. So as much as possible, I make myself work, even when it feels impossible. I always have to remind myself that there has *never* been a situation where I felt better if I didn't get something done.

- There are many days I want to substitute mindless behavior for actual work. But I've learned that the feeling I get after getting something done is often far superior to watching a bad DVD or some other pointless task.

- I have some days when I have trouble focusing my thoughts because of depression. I just have to feel this, accept it, and move on. I try to keep away from busy work such as paying bills on these days and focus on my writing.

Exercise

What depression symptoms make it difficult for you to get things done? Write them down here:

_____

_____

_____

_____

_____

Memorize this list—write it down and carry it with you if you need to—and recall it on the days when having a normal life seems impossible. By knowing this list, you can actually compare your current thoughts with those of the past to realistically remind yourself that you always feel this way when you're depressed and that you can get things done.

ASK DR. PRESTON

 Why are some people able to work and get on with life despite being very depressed?

 Clearly, some people struggle with enormous amounts of depression and yet keep functioning. Take Abraham Lincoln, for example. Some people are able to transcend their own suffering. This seems to be what he did; the need to lead his country outweighed his frequent urge to commit suicide. Find a purpose that engages your body and mind, like Lincoln and his country. You might be surprised how very much that helps.

Life Goes on, Even with Depression

A further note from Julie: Feeling the depression and doing it anyway changed my life. I keep trying to work through my depression because I want to reach my dreams. There's nothing I won't do to stay alive. I want to see my nephew grow up. I want to feel romantic love. I want to travel and maybe go to school like a normal person. I have dreams despite being depressed most of the time. Getting things done no matter how hard it is or how terrible I feel comes from an inner strength we *all* have. Maybe you'll cry all through the day, but you have it in you to keep going. You just have to tap into that strength by sheer determination.

Here are some other thoughts to consider:

- Depression, like many other disabilities, might be present all the time, but it doesn't define who you are or what you can accomplish.

- When depression makes you hopeless, do something you know will give you hope—even if it's just a sliver of hope.

- When you wake up depressed, say to yourself, *Darn it, I'm depressed again, but just as if I had a broken leg, I will get up and get on with my day.*

- Expect to cry, feel terrible, be less productive, and feel like quitting … and then do what you have to do anyway.

- Whether you have chronic depression or periodic depression, you will have days when you have to get things done no matter how you feel. It may help to think of Abraham Lincoln. He's proof that it is possible, despite feeling very depressed, that you can do what you have to do.

Remember: Feel the depression and do it anyway so you can at least wake up the next day knowing you accomplished something under very difficult circumstances. You absolutely can get things done, even when you're depressed.

Finish School

School creates unique challenges when a person is depressed. The deadlines are often more intense than a traditional work environment, and the amount of information that needs to be digested and tested can feel overwhelming. And if you come from a family that holds education in high esteem, you've likely got additional pressure and high expectations. Even when you're not depressed, that can be a lot to deal with.

Why Is School So Difficult?

School often encompasses all the individual situations that can be difficult for someone who is depressed, but when they're combined, they can be almost overwhelming for a person who's depressed. Large, overstimulating classrooms; changes in eating and sleep patterns; living with strangers; heavy reading; intense concentration; public (class) speaking; test taking; keeping to a very strict time schedule; thinking of the future; increase in alcohol consumption; being away from parents for the first time; feeling isolated; working while going to school—that's a lot, but it's not even all of the pressures students often have to deal with. These changes are very intense for some students, who have little preparation for the extra mental problems outside of their actual class work.

When you're depressed, having human contact can often feel a lot better than sitting alone and cramming yourself with information. But considering that you're in school to learn skills, get a degree, and (for most people) get a job, you must create a school structure that supports you even when you feel too sick to study and attend class.

Do any of these potential school problems apply to you?

- Taking on too many classes/pushing yourself too hard.
- Getting involved in stressful relationships.
- Feeling unprepared for the reality of college life.
- Feeling overwhelmed by dorms, people around campus, the fast-paced life, and large classes.

- Unable to finish course work due to depression.
- Feeling lethargic either from the depression or depression medications.

Raymond's Story

I started law school at age 22, and I was very pleased and excited to get into a top university. The first year wasn't so bad, but by the second year, my depression was getting worse and worse and I had trouble focusing in class. The topics that were pretty easy the first year became more and more difficult to understand as my depression grew worse. I remember sitting in a lecture, crying, worried that I would flunk out. I had trouble in my study groups and started sleeping when I should have been studying. My adviser suggested I see a doctor. I kept thinking I was doing something wrong and that my intellect and sheer determination were enough to get me through. They weren't.

I saw the doctor, and he agreed that I was profoundly depressed and suggested I take some time off. This isn't really a possibility in law school. I would be behind in my classes and miss taking the "baby bars" on schedule. But I had no choice once I started to miss classes. It was a really hard decision, especially for my parents, who were paying my living expenses. But I knew I had to do something.

So I took a year off. I went on antidepressants, took a very low-paying social services job, and started to get better. When the year was over, I went back to class with more hope, but knew I had to be prepared. For the next two years of school, I was depressed off and on, but I was more able to handle it due to the medications and my time off.

I'm now a lawyer. Yes, taking a year off did mess up my schedule. But without that year off, I don't think I would have finished at all. I may have taken a lot more time to finish than other students, but I'm glad I stuck it out.

My Story

I went to college before I created the strategies in this book. It took me eight years to get a degree. My family emphasizes education over almost anything else, and I was constantly asked why I couldn't just get my degree and then my Master's and Ph.D. like I should. "You are so smart, Julie, you could be a lawyer or professor or anything you want if you could just settle down and get your degrees."

I definitely feel sad about the time lost and the fact that I was often too depressed and or distracted to keep going with my education. But I now see it as a miracle that I got my degree. Few areas in my life haven't been affected by depression, but losing my ability to go to school in a normal amount of time has been a major disappointment.

What I do now:

- Accept that going to school full-time is not an option for me.

- I have a rule that I finish classes. Period.

- I audit classes so I don't feel too overwhelmed.

- I try to face the facts: I'm in my 40s, and getting a Ph.D. anytime soon is probably not a reality—especially considering that I don't have a Master's degree yet!

Exercise

On the tough days, remind yourself that you're working toward a very specific goal—graduation. If you need to, write down your school start and finish dates so you always have them at hand. You can remind yourself of these dates when it seems like school will go on forever and you will never graduate.

Your start date: _____

Your finish date: _____

The time is going to pass anyway, so you might as well get an education. You'll get your degree if you stick to it.

ASK DR. PRESTON

Q **Why is school so difficult for depressed people?**

A Depression can cause impaired concentration and ability to think, which can result in poor grades. Then, the poor grades cause increasing feelings of failure and low self-esteem. In addition, the social requirements at school may become a source of distress, as the depressed person can often become isolated from people.

Create a Structure and Keep Going

Many people go to college at a young age right out of high school. They are often away from family and the everyday structure they knew as children. If you were depressed before going to school, it's especially important that you remind yourself that school can be a depression trigger and plan accordingly. If you're in school now and the depression is new, you can create a structure you can use for school as well as your future work years. It'll all be worth it; the day you have your degree will be one of the proudest days of your life.

Here are some more tips for getting your degree:

School has a set start and finish date. Degrees end. It helps if you constantly remind yourself that what you're going through is not forever and that you can hold out if you think of the finished goal—a degree—instead of focusing on the amount of work you have to do now.

The work you do when you're depressed is often as good as the work you do when you're well. This seems impossible when you're in the middle of a project, but it's often true. When the negative thoughts come up that your work is no good, counteract them with specific replies such as *I will keep going. The work has to get done, and I'll simply do what I can.*

There's no question that depression physically affects brain function. If you feel more distracted and less open to new information when you're depressed, you're not imagining things. You have solution options. For some, antidepressants and ADHD-type medications help. For others, overriding the depression and working anyway does the trick.

Rethink your expectations. Are your standards for when you're well simply not possible when you're depressed?

Ask for help. In many schools, teaching assistants have time to help you with difficult courses. You can go for help every day.

Never quit. Unless you are truly too depressed to work—which means you need immediate professional help—you have to make a rule for yourself that you won't quit in the middle of a class. Finishing is often just as important as a grade.

But don't let your class load get out of control. You might not be able to handle a full class load. This can be frustrating, but remember, you have to focus on the end goal, getting a degree, instead of getting down on yourself for not being able to handle a full load like many of your classmates. Ask yourself what's more important, a degree or getting perfect grades. Some students with depression have to make that decision daily.

Always go to class. This is not negotiable. Even if you sit in the back of the class crying, go to class. You'll always feel better if you go, because depression responds to rules. Your brain is chaotic when you're depressed, so you have to work around this and create structure.

And finally, the most important thing is to have a time and set place for studying. First decide what type of environment works best for you to take in information. The library? A coffee shop? Your dorm? Next, set a time and place to study, and make it non-negotiable. That means setting limits to any possible distractions. You might have to find a space where there are no people you know. You might have to turn off your cell phone, ban yourself from e-mail, and *make* yourself sit down and get your work done. If you think about it, this is really the only way you can make it through school: you have to sit down and study.

Remember: Anyone who gets a degree while dealing with depression is a true scholar.

Talk Back to Depression

A depressed brain constantly tells you what you're doing wrong, which is one of the main reasons you can't get things done when you're depressed. The tug-of-war struggle between what you want and need to do versus what depression is telling you to do can take away all your energy. With no energy, you don't get anything done. You then feel terrible for not getting anything done … and the cycle starts all over again.

Depression's negative chatter can be very, very persuasive. It's hard to maintain who you are when you hear a barrage of negative self-talk all day long. But you don't have to listen. Confront the thoughts depression gives you, and show depression who's boss.

Take Back the Power

You'd probably never let a real person talk to you the way depression talks to you. You would fight back; you'd say, "Leave me alone!" or "You're hurting me!" No matter what personality you have when faced with adversaries, remember that depression can so completely take over your thoughts that you're no longer able to function at work or at home. This is especially true if you believe what the thoughts tell you.

Talking back to depression gives you the power. It can snap you back to reality and help you stay in the moment instead of letting depression lead you on a path through your "miserable" past and "hopeless" future.

Why do you need to talk back to depression?

- Depression controls your thoughts.
- Depression is scary and wants to hurt you.
- Depression tells you what to do.
- Depression is not a positive companion.
- Depression is a bully.

There's no question that depression can be very mean. You can counteract this by saying no and then being good to yourself.

Mary's Story

I've been depressed for all of my adult life. I've felt like a failure for years. Whenever I'd try to do something, I'd get flooded by negative words and feelings. *You can't do this. You're crazy. You'll never get anything done.* I felt a terrible feeling of doom. I got overwhelmed, and it really did just seem easier to sit and do nothing. But the day would pass with my accomplishing nothing, and I was more miserable than when I sat down. It's like someone was abusing me, and I just sat there and took it. *There's no point in living like this. Your life gives you no pleasure. There's no point in going on today.*

Finally I just couldn't take it anymore. I didn't have a job or any money. I was always sick. One day, I told my depressed thoughts to just shut up. I said, "Shut up! I won't listen." I got up from the chair, and I changed. It took more than a year to learn to see these thoughts for what they were and fight back, but now I don't let depression tell me what to do. I still hear what it says, but I don't have to believe it anymore. I just say, "Shut up!"

My Story

I will never let depression take over my life like it did for more than 20 years. I'm in control now, and I remind depression of that all the time. I often see depression like a monster at my door. Sometimes I can make it leave by saying "No, you are not welcome here!" At other times it gets in the door and it's harder to deal with, but I never stop talking to it. "Leave me alone. You aren't real. Don't say those things, because they aren't true. This isn't the real me. I will work today. I will not listen to you." It's very tiring, and sometimes I have to do this all day, but I'm often able to kick it out the door.

What I do now:

- I know what depression sounds like. I know what is real and isn't real.

- I know that I will still lose days to the depression. I will get despondent and won't write, and my house will get messy, and I *will* feel like a failure. That's how it is.

- I talk to depression out loud. It's sometimes more effective than my internal voice.

Exercise

Imagine yourself on a playground. You're there doing your thing and a bully comes up and starts yelling at you and pushing you around. The bully says things you know aren't true, but they still hurt. You may feel angry, shocked, worried, or scared, but you feel helpless in the face of the attack. You wonder, *Why is this person doing this to me? I haven't done anything to them! And the things they're saying aren't really true!*

When you're faced with this attack, you have two options. You can run away with the knowledge that the bully will probably follow because he or she likes the smell of fear. Or you can stand firm, look the bully in the face, and say, "You don't scare me. These things are not true. I will not listen to you!"

Bullies are rarely the strong ones. Like depression, they attack for no real reason and keep attacking until something talks back. Depression is your bully. Talk back to depression and tell it you are not scared and it needs to leave you alone.

The next time depression bullies you, what are you going to say? Write it here:

_____

_____

_____

_____

_____

ASK DR. PRESTON

Q **Why are depressive thoughts so mean?**

A Many people who experience depression have a critical inner voice. Often this is a result of parents who were harsh. The child comes to believe, on a deep level, that he or she is bad, worthless, ashamed, or undeserving of love. These chronic feelings of low self-esteem and worthlessness almost always become intensified during bouts of depression.

Always Talk Back

Talking back to depression helps you realize that the thoughts you have *are not real* and you can counteract them with your real thoughts. When you learn to recognize the depression thoughts, you can say no to them and move on with your day. And when they keep coming at you, just keep saying no!

Here's what you can say when depression is being a bully:

- "I won't listen."
- "This is my life."
- "I choose to do something today."
- "I don't argue with my own brain. I make my own decisions."
- "Shut up and leave me alone!"

Here are some other thoughts to consider:

- Walk away with purpose. Get up and do something even when the thoughts and desperate feelings are raging.
- Accept that your brain may be filled with chatter and negative thoughts, but you can still get on with your project.
- Remind yourself that bullies don't speak the truth, and neither does depression.

Remember: Talking back to depression might seem a bit odd—it's like talking to the air or to yourself. But who cares, as long as it works?

17

Set Time Limits

Have you ever noticed that depression can distort time? It's really good at making a day seem like a year that will never end. You may look at your watch and think, *Only five more hours until I can get into bed.* On other days, the day might rush by and you realize you've done absolutely nothing.

A lot of this has to do with the fact that depression tells you that you can't complete projects anyway, which makes you not even try to focus on the amount of time you have to get something done.

The Chess Match

If you've ever seen a chess match, you know that each player's move is timed. And for good reason. When you have unlimited time to think, you often take as much time as possible to ponder all the possibilities.

But with a depressed brain, that unlimited time could easily stretch to forever. It may take forever—or at least feel like it—to do something. But the depressed brain won't devote that much time to something and will likely quit well before the "something" ever gets done.

The solution is to set time limits for specific projects. Setting time limits is different from time management. It's more small scale, like specific project micromanagement. On depressed days, micromanaging your time is not a bad idea. In fact, your brain often responds to the time limits with relief.

Here are some signs you need time limits:

- You feel very scattered and unfocused.
- Things either don't get done or take a lot longer than they would take if you were not depressed.
- You feel overwhelmed with projects, so you don't do any of them on time.
- You're unable to conceptualize the time it takes to do certain projects.
- You waste time instead of using time to your advantage.

Depression seems to take away your ability to control your time. You can take back that control.

Anna's Story

Something really weird happens to time when I'm depressed. It slows down almost to a minute-by-minute feeling. I think, *Three hours until lunch. Six hours until I can go get into bed.* I measure it that exactly. Yet when it comes to school, when I know I have to write a paper by a certain time or get ready for a class, I feel like I don't have enough time!

On one hand, I feel the time creeping by and that my life is pointless; on the other, I feel rushed and overwhelmed by the short amount of time I have to do my work. This is definitely relativity at work!

I've found that the only way to deal with this is have external timers. Friends are my biggest help. They check in on me and say, "It's been one hour—what have you done?" and then "I'll be back in two hours." It calms me down because they take control of my time so I don't have to.

My Story

I think that one of the reasons I never was able to complete the projects I really wanted to finish is because I had no idea how to break them down. I saw time as a big blob. I focused on how long a project would take overall, instead of focusing on the fact that most projects can be broken into sections that can easily be timed.

I once had a business coach tell me to write down all the things I had to do in a day, rank them by importance, and then get very strict with how much time I would spend on each project. I had to think about how long I was allowed to be on e-mail and how long I could make calls. I had to time my lunch and coffee breaks. And I wasn't allowed to go to the next project until the first one was done. I realized that by limiting my time on each project, I actually had more time.

Time has too many implications in depression. It takes my time, ruins my time, and makes it difficult for me to see the reality of how much time something actually takes. I used to either take too long and miss deadlines or not do something at all. Now I can at least look at my timed list and see what I've been doing all day and if I got anything done.

What I do now:

- I think of the amount of time I have to do something and then make sure I know how long each section will take. On my well days this just comes naturally, but on the days I'm depressed, I have to make a point to do this constantly.

- I focus on making my publishing deadlines even when I'm ill. Having someone else set the timeline helps me immensely. I actually focus better and feel less pressure when I know exactly when something is due.

- I set limits on how long I'm allowed to talk on the phone when I'm working. I do feel like I need to talk to my friends and family when I'm working, but I don't really. I allow myself to talk on a break and then I say, "Well, I have to get back to work. I'll call you later." And on the days when I'm super-distracted, I limit my time on the phone to zero!

Exercise

To use the chess metaphor again, when a player makes a move, he or she then hits a clock that records the time he or she took to make a decision. So a game has a certain number of moves in an allotted period of time.

You can do the same for yourself. Write out what you have to do and put a time next to each step; estimate how long each step will take if you have to. Note the time you start a project, work on it until you finish, and then note the time you stopped. Don't go on to the next step until you've completed the first one.

ASK DR. PRESTON

Q **Why does setting very specific project time limits help a person with depression?**

A Avoiding situations that can intensify feelings of powerlessness is an ongoing concern for people who are depressed. It's so common for a depressed person to have unproductive days and then later reflect on the day and conclude that they got nothing done. That reflecting only heightens their feelings of low self-esteem and the perception of being out of control of their lives.

Establishing personal goals and deadlines can be helpful, especially if the tasks are broken down into small, timed chunks that are realistically attainable. Accomplishing smaller tasks during the day and then checking them off the list can be a good reality check. The person can see what they've accomplished and have physical proof something got done, which can combat some of their overwhelmed and powerless feelings.

The Depressed Brain Is Not a Good Timer

A depressed brain distorts time, and there's no way it's going to help you time your work efficiently without some outside help. Having a physical measurement of time can help you complete tasks. For example, the sound of an alarm keeps you in the moment so you can control time more effectively, and deadlines can take away the pressure and help you focus on what you have to do instead of how long it will take.

Here are some other thoughts to consider:

- Use a watch or cell phone alarm to time specific projects and then set a rule with yourself that you will not get up until the alarm goes off.

- Ask a friend to call you after a set amount of time.

- Use outside time limits set by authority figures such as a boss, a teacher, or a member of an organization.

- Be aware of how long something *should* take so you can have more realistic start and finish times.

Remember: Depression has a timeline called forever (often known as never!). You'll always have to impose your time schedule on your projects when you're depressed.

_18_

Expect to Be Physically Uncomfortable

It's very common for your body to feel out of sorts when you're depressed. Sitting at a desk or in a meeting can feel excruciating when your brain isn't functioning properly. When a task in front of you requires focus or quiet, it can be hard to keep still and feel grounded enough to finish your work. Restless legs, nervousness, and even back- or headaches can all be a result of depression. These can all significantly affect your ability to do the things you want to do.

Why Does Depression Feel So Physical?

Depression is often accompanied by anxiety. Anxiety can manifest as discomfort in your body and can even make you feel like you're having a heart attack. If not recognized early enough, anxiety can lead to significant discomfort that then makes it nearly impossible for you to focus on what you have to do. Anxiety can feel like you're going to pop out of your skin, which is why it needs to be recognized and treated along with your depression.

In addition, the brain chemicals that cause depression don't only affect the brain; they can affect your physical body as well. So when you're depressed, it's not only your brain that goes through changes.

It's important that you're aware of your body when you're depressed. Depression makes you feel uncomfortable and can also slow or speed up your reflexes to a point where you can hurt yourself. When you remember that depression is not only a mental illness but a physical illness as well, you can pay attention to what you need to do to keep your body healthy and more comfortable.

Have you experienced any of these physical signs of depression?

- You trip or fall more than usual or have trouble going down stairs.
- Your muscles are tired or restless.
- You have trouble sitting at a desk.

- You toss and turn when you're trying to sleep.
- Your breathing and heartbeat are rapid due to anxiety.

Remain aware of your body when you're depressed so you can decide what is a real discomfort and what is something you just have to work through.

Marilyn's Story

When I'm depressed, my face feels really funny and itchy. I tend to touch my chin and eyebrows a lot and can't seem to get comfortable. I work in a library, and sometimes it just makes me want to scream if I have to sit another hour. But I have to. It's hard enough to be depressed and worry all day about my job and whether I need to go get my library sciences Master's and whether I'll be promoted, but adding the physical stuff is painful. On some days, my ribs hurt and I can feel all the bones in my body ache. I twist and turn, the chair feels hard, and I can't keep my back straight.

When I'm not depressed, I like my job and the quiet. My thoughts are about work, not about how physically uncomfortable I am. On restless days, I try to contract my muscles and get exercise in that way, even though I'm sitting. I can stretch my legs under my desk as well, and I always take the stairs when I can.

My Story

I have some days when I'm depressed and my legs hurt. My clothes feel too heavy. Sometimes my hair really bothers my neck, and my face feels funny. I twist my back a lot and feel hyperaware of all the pains in my body. I used to attribute this to something from outside me, such as an allergy or a lack of exercise, but I finally realized that depression simply makes me antsy and uncomfortable. This has a lot to do with anxiety. I often feel that something is pushing me from behind. On the really bad days, I actually feel I'm going to burst out of my skin if I don't get up and move. I fidget a lot. I used to be a serious hypochondriac because I thought the physical pain I felt was the sign of something really serious. It never was.

What I do now:

- I'm careful to look where I'm walking. I've twisted my ankles so many times when I was depressed, I don't want it to happen again.

- I get a massage or get in a hot tub.

- I make deals with myself. *Finish editing this section, Julie, and you can get up and stretch.* I just did this with the chapter you're reading now. At this point my elbows hurt. I have a mild headache. I was crying this morning and feel a bit worn out. I feel a lot of tension in my back, and I don't want to be at this desk writing. But I keep going because I have to.

- I live with the pain instead of focusing on it to the point that I can't sit.

Exercise

Often, you're unaware of just how physical depression can be until you make a list of what you feel physically when you're depressed. For example, old injuries might hurt more, your arthritis might flare up, you might get more frequent headaches, etc. Depression might also cause you to have more accidents: maybe you tripped on a curb and fell into traffic, got startled by a barking dog and twisted your ankle, or hit another car because your reflexes were so slow.

What are your physical signs of depression? List them here:

Physical symptoms:

_____

_____

_____

_____

_____

Accidents:

_____

_____

_____

_____

_____

The more aware you are of how depression affects you physically, the better prepared and safer you can be.

ASK DR. PRESTON

Q Why is the depressed person's body so uncomfortable?

A Depression can be accompanied by a number of stress-related physical problems, especially tension headaches and constipation. Plus, depression can disrupt sleep, which can lower pain thresholds, which, in turn, can increase pain. Fatigue is a primary depressive symptom and is almost always felt as a source of physical discomfort.

Treat the Depression, End the Discomfort

Uncomfortable physical problems caused by depression can go away when the depression is being treated successfully. It's also important that you move your body, take care of it, and focus on work instead of how you physically feel. If someone has ever said to you, "You sure are antsy," "You seem to go to the doctor a lot," or "Careful—you get into a lot of accidents," listen to these statements and let them be a sign that maybe depression is causing physical problems that need your attention.

Here are some other thoughts to consider:

- Exercise in the morning.
- Force yourself to stay in one place no matter how you feel.
- Notice if you're pacing and not getting anything done.
- Stretch and do yoga at your desk. (Don't worry, no one is watching!)
- Avoid too much caffeine or being too hungry.
- Be sure an antidepressant is not causing the physically uncomfortable feelings.
- Watch your posture while you work.
- Walk, run, or go to an exercise class during lunch.

Remember: Uncomfortable physical problems and accidents are an unfortunate part of depression. The more aware you are of your body, the safer and more comfortable you can be.

Ah, now I can get up and take a walk!

Just Sit Down

On some days, the act of sitting down in front of a project can be just what you need to keep going. You can say to yourself, *I'm just going to sit. That's the first step. I don't have to do anything more. Then I will move my hands and type, or make a sales call.*

When you're depressed, you can feel like a hand is physically holding you back from sitting down and starting something. It can feel like you're fighting with an unseen force. *It's just sitting,* you might say to yourself, but when your brain is misfiring and you're having trouble making decisions, feel uncomfortable, and want to cry, sitting down is a big accomplishment.

Sitting—That's Easy, Right?

What's the big deal about sitting down to get something done? Sitting is easy, right? But it's often more than just sitting. Sitting down in front of a project—whether it be artistic, sales oriented, or working with a child's homework—can be daunting. It's often much easier to put off projects until they are so backed up they never get done. But no more! From now on, tell yourself you *will* commit to sitting and go from there. Sitting down when you need to often triggers a work response that helps you get things done.

Are any of these signs you need to sit down familiar to you?

- Pacing or wandering aimlessly.
- Getting coffee you don't need.
- Talking with others.
- Feeling so overwhelmed by an entire project that you don't start at all.
- Avoiding the location of the project like the plague.

Michael's Story

I have actually walked around my office for hours without sitting down for an extended period of time. There is my office chair; I can see it looming at me. In fact, my whole office is a scary space. I tell myself, *Just sit down and get started,* yet I still keep walking around, getting coffee, talking with colleagues, copying stuff I don't need.

But now I have a rule. When I get to work, the first thing I do is go into my office and sit in my chair for three hours. I have my coffee with me, and I tell people I can chat when my time is up. Once I've sat down, the work goes easier and I find it a lot easier to stay seated throughout the day.

My Story

I lost years of work because I couldn't do something as simple as sitting down in a chair in front of a project. I could sit in chairs in restaurants and on airplanes—those chairs that had nothing to do with work—but chairs that represented work were another story.

After I thought about it, I realized that sitting down in a chair isn't really the problem. The problem must be what the chair represents. I determined that I see the sitting as the first step in a project that my brain has told me I can't do. That's why sitting down is so hard.

What I do now:

- I constantly remind myself that if I just sit down in front of something, it can kick-start my desire to do my work.

- I know for a fact that getting myself to my office space and sitting in my chair gets me going when I'm sick.

- I make sure the chair is comfortable!

Exercise

What projects do you do that require you to sit down and focus? These can include art as well as work or school projects:

Studying for a test	Writing an article
Practicing the piano	Reading to a child
Working on the computer	Finishing an art project

Write your own here:

_____

_____

_____

_____

_____

The next time you're faced with the project, remind yourself that you only have to do the first step—you have to sit. Sitting down is often enough to get you started.

ASK DR. PRESTON

Q **Why does taking the very small step of sitting in front of a project help get things done?**

A A depressed person can waste so much time just thinking about having to do something that the time passes and nothing is accomplished. This is where people often get bogged down the most.

Depressed people often have an image of what they need to do, and when they take stock of their currently available energy and motivation, the conclusion is too often, *Why even try?* By sitting down to start a project, though, a person makes the decision to work one step at a time. This is especially true when people break down a big task (*My whole house is a mess*) into smaller chunks (*I can clean off the coffee table*).

So much of this has to do with what psychologist Albert Banbura called "one's appraisal of self-efficacy." A person asks, *In my mind, in this moment, how much confidence do I have in being able to cope with the task (or the stressors) currently facing me?* When the conclusion is positive (*I can do this … it isn't unmanageable*), it often ignites some internal energy and enthusiasm that's then used to initiate action: sitting down and getting started. And with ongoing task completion, the depressed person receives ongoing feedback (*Yes … I am making headway*), which helps sustain activity.

Take the First Step

If you have work that requires sitting, you have to take the first step and *sit*. That might mean sitting at a desk in your house or an office or going to a meeting or getting in a car. But the more you get used to sitting as a first step, the more you can use this small movement to help you get on with your task.

Sitting represents ...

- Making a choice.
- Facing work that feels overwhelming and difficult.
- Entering work mode.
- Respect for yourself.
- Control over your behavior even when depression is raging.

Remember: Sit. Sit. Sit. That's all you have to do to get started.

Know When Your Brain Is Lying to You

When depression takes over your thoughts, your thoughts start to tell you lies. It's easy to get caught up in these lies because they seem so real. *How can they not be real?* you wonder. *They come from my head. I must think this way, and my thoughts must be true.*

In reality, depression makes you think many, many things that aren't true—often they're not even *partially* true. If you listen to these thoughts, they can take over your day and sometimes your life and make it difficult to do what you need to do. And sometimes the thoughts are such outrageous lies that you might cause considerable problems when you make choices based on those wrong thoughts.

Can Your Brain Really Lie?

It might seem odd to think your brain is lying to you, but facts are facts. If your brain says you've never gotten anything done and it's obvious you've done many things throughout your life, then the thought is obviously a lie. You can't always depend on your brain to work properly and lead you to thoughts that are real when you're depressed. The thoughts can be very, very wrong, and if you act on them, you can easily sabotage the work you're currently doing as well as future projects.

When these thoughts start, ask yourself, *Are these really my thoughts? If I ignore what my brain is saying and actually examine my thoughts to find the reality of the situation, can I get the project done?* And then think of how the well you would talk to the depressed you, and you're on your way to counteracting the lies.

Has your brain told you any of these lies?

- *I'll never be able to work like other people.*
- *I'm a terrible father/mother/spouse.*
- *My house is never clean.*
- *I can't do even the smallest jobs.*

- *I'm a quitter.*
- *I'll never be able to finish this project.*

Richard's Story

I have a hard time distinguishing the real me from the depressed me. I often wonder how it's possible that depression mimics my voice, my thoughts, and my actions, but totally distorts and twists them into something that's not me.

It's like being in a the scene from the movie *Enter the Dragon* where Bruce Lee is in a room of broken mirrors. No matter where he looks, he sees an image of what looks real, but in reality, there's only one true image. He can't tell where the bad guy is. He's guessing and has his hands out in front of him in a kung fu stance, and he just can't tell what to do!

That's what it's like for me. All these images look the same, but only one is the real me. I get lost in the whole thing. Do I really hate myself that much? I think it would be a bit easier to hear someone saying these things about me out loud because I could at least be more objective. I could say, "That's not true. This person just doesn't like me."

It took me a long time to learn how to deal with the lies my brain bombarded me with. I did learn, though. When I have a totally mean thought about myself now, such as *You're the worst worker in the office and people only keep you around because they have to,* I really examine where the thought's coming from. I used to think it was lack of self-esteem, but it's not! I truly don't think this way when I'm well. I believe in my work. So I now know what a brain lie sounds like and I talk back. *This is not true,* I tell myself. *The real me doesn't feel this. I don't have to listen to this. It's a lie.* It's all about awareness.

My Story

I listened to the thoughts manufactured by my brain from age 14 to 35 and thought they were real. Even when the evidence pointed to the opposite, I believed what I heard in my head simply because it was my own head! No one else was talking in there. Or so I thought.

When I started to treat my depression, I noticed that these thoughts had a pattern. When I was faced with a job that felt too big, my brain told me it was too big and then listed all the reasons I would never get it finished. I would get excited when I had an idea for something and then it would just fizzle out, and I would move on to something new. I've always wanted to write self-help books, but I never got past outlining the original idea. The thoughts were just too strong.

Many people might think I had low self-esteem and I just didn't believe in myself. This might be the case for some people, but not for me. If that were true, then all the self-help books I read and therapists I saw for 20 years would have helped me get things done. Nothing really helped until I finally realized that my brain was wrong.

What I do now:

- I know for a fact that I can get things done, even when my brain is very forcefully telling me I can't.

- When I'm depressed, I still have the exact same thoughts I had when I was 14. I just don't believe them anymore.

- There are definitely a lot of days when the thoughts take over and the lies seem 100 percent real. I even tell them to other people. I've taught my friends and family to remind me, "You're depressed, Julie. Those thoughts are not true." This helps me see the truth: I'm depressed and my brain is once again telling lies.

Exercise

What lies does your depressed brain tell you? List them here:

_____

_____

_____

_____

_____

Do the thoughts have a pattern? Often brain lies fall into categories such as management skills, parenting skills, interacting with others, being on time, cooking, etc. What makes these lies so difficult to notice and counteract is that your brain knows and takes advantage of your weak spots. If you had a thought such as, *You're a terrible cook and dinner is never on time,* and yet cooking is not something you're particularly concerned about, the thought isn't powerful. But if you're a chef and you start having thoughts about your cooking and work skills, this can be profoundly disturbing and may even make you doubt your work.

ASK DR. PRESTON

Q **Why does the depressed brain lie to people?**

A Some scientists think a major factor that causes and makes depression worse is a perceptual bias. When confronted with the facts, depressed people are very likely to notice the negative things in others, in themselves, and in the world in general.

This also applies to their views of the future. They don't see the future in terms of possibilities but rather see a future clouded by negative bias. In the depressed person's world, the future looks hopeless, and pessimism abounds. Negative conclusions such as *I can't do anything right* or *No one will ever love me* are taken as fact, when in reality these might not be accurate conclusions at all. Strongly held negative beliefs often pervasively color every moment and are a major contributor to ongoing depressed moods.

Finding the Truth

If you've been depressed a long time, it's possible you've been conditioned to listen to and believe the thoughts your depressed brain feeds you. You have to recondition yourself to notice the difference between the truthful things your well brain says and the lies your depressed brain tells you.

Here are some other thoughts to consider:

- Notice if you're having patently untrue or outrageous thoughts and then see them for what they are: lies.
- Refuse to negotiate with a liar, especially when it's your own brain.
- Say, "You're lying," out loud and refuse to listen.
- Don't believe everything you think!

Remember: Ben Franklin said, "Who has deceiv'd thee so oft as thy self?" When you're depressed, the real question is, "What has deceiv'd thee so oft as thy brain?"

Don't Worry About Something, *Do* Something

It's much easier to get things done than worry about *not* getting things done. This might sound very simplistic, but the absolutely best way to get out of an *I-can't-do-anything* mood is simply to do something. Thinking and stressing about all you're not getting done takes a lot more energy than getting up and just doing the dishes, creating a presentation, or taking a walk.

Make a Deal with Yourself

Right now, make a deal with yourself that you'll do what you need to do today so when the worrying and obsessing starts over what you're not getting done, you'll see it as a sign that depression is thinking for you and it's time for the real you to take over.

The depressed brain will always tell you that it takes much longer to do something than it actually does. It's always off base. It can also make you dread something you know you have to do on a regular basis, even the smallest things such as taking out the garbage. You think, *Oh no, I have to do it again. I hate this. I just can't do this today.* You're not only setting yourself up to avoid a project, but you're also ensuring that the project will be difficult when you finally do get around to it.

The day you realize that it takes a lot less time to do something than to worry about it is the day you can increase your productivity 100 percent.

What do you consistently put off in your life?

- Paying the bills?
- Planning a business trip?
- Cleaning the house?
- Going to the store?
- Getting ready for a presentation at work?
- Finishing a commission?

Think of the worry factor and then the time it actually takes to do something. Which choice is more constructive?

Arlene's Story

Cleaning my house feels impossible when I'm depressed. Literally impossible. I don't even want to walk into the kitchen. If someone asked me how long I thought it would take to clean my house I would have said six or seven hours. Talk about distortion! Instead of facing this six or seven hours (I now know this estimate is way off), I would get more upset as my house got messier and messier. *Look at me,* I would think, *I can't even keep my house clean.* It was way too overwhelming.

Then one day I couldn't take it anymore and I *forced* myself to walk into the kitchen and do one thing. It would feel exhausting, but I always felt better afterward. Then I would have to sit down for a bit before I could get up and do one more thing. I realized that I can easily clean my entire house in two hours.

It can take longer on the days when I'm depressed; actually, on those days I just do a little at a time. But at least the kitchen gets done. And it hardly takes any time at all. I always feel better when I wake up to a clean house.

My Story

I've been depressed off and on for weeks (nothing new for me), and it's very easy for me to think about writing this book and how I'm behind and how it will be a mess and no one will like it and it won't help anyone and it's too hard ... *Wait a minute!*

Thinking this way takes a *lot* of energy with no reward. Sitting down and writing a paragraph takes little energy and actually has huge rewards—that paragraph.

What I do now:

- I often get angry with myself and say, *Walk over there and put up your clothes. It will take you about five minutes. You've been upset about these clothes for weeks. This is stupid!*

- I know how long things take so I'm not totally overwhelmed when faced with a task.

- If I'm obsessing about something and how I need to do it, I have to make myself stop and think and rationally talk to myself about how getting it done is easier than worrying about it.

Exercise

What projects do you consistently worry about not getting done to the point that the stress is often worse than the project itself? Focus on one project and then …

1. Write what you think about when faced with this project.
2. Think about the time it actually takes to do the project and compare that to how much time you spend worrying about the project.
3. Write how you feel if you put off the project.
4. Describe what it feels like once the project is done.

For example, here's one of mine:

Answering e-mail: I really hate keeping up with all my e-mail. It never seems to stop, and it takes up so much of my day. I've been putting off answering my e-mail for weeks now, and I feel terrible. I think it will take me at least four to five hours to get caught up. I have hundreds of e-mails. I hate thinking about this all the time. I feel over-whelmed. My e-mail feels like a monster in my computer.

Now for the reality: Actually, I can get all my e-mail done in less than an hour per day. The problem is when I put it off for days and then I can't sleep and feel stupid and depressed. I feel so much better when I see the clean inbox. So much better!

When you know you have a tendency to worry more about projects than actually doing them, you can look for this behavior every time something feels difficult and the worrying starts.

ASK DR. PRESTON

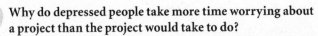

Q Why do depressed people take more time worrying about a project than the project would take to do?

A People who are depressed are often plagued with self-doubt. They lack the confidence that they'll be able to be effective in whatever tasks they take on, and they predict failure in all they do. Anticipation of failure or the belief that their efforts will be in vain can lead to procrastination. Procrastination then fuels the fires of low self-esteem, and it all becomes a vicious cycle. It makes sense that a depressed person puts off something they've estimated to take much more time than it really does. The fact that depression can also result in very low energy also adds to the problem.

Lose the Worry

When you're worried and thinking way too much about not getting things done, ask yourself realistically how long a project will take and then think of the time you've spent worrying about it. Now think about how you'll feel when you get it done and especially how accomplished you'll feel when you go to bed at night. This should make your choice of what to do a lot more clear.

Did you know ...

- It takes about three minutes to unload a dishwasher.
- Answering e-mail usually takes about a quarter of the time you think it will.
- Making one sales call is a lot quicker than thinking of all of the calls you have to make.
- Cleaning the bathroom takes less than 20 minutes.
- Going to the store can be really quick if you have a list.
- Cleaning an entire house usually takes about an hour and a half.
- Getting ready for a presentation at work almost always takes less time to actually do than the time you take worrying about whether you can do it.

Remember: The time spent worrying about what you have to do simply doesn't equal the time it takes to do the project. Save yourself some time and do the project.

Regulate Your Sleep

Sleep helps regulate the brain chemicals that control your emotions, and as a result, the amount of sleep you get can significantly affect your depression in a positive or negative way. Regular sleep patterns set what's known as the body's *circadian rhythm,* and when you get enough sleep, you wake up refreshed instead of having to fight tiredness and low productivity the rest of the day.

Circadian rhythm refers to the internal body clock that helps you maintain the 24-hour cycle of brain activity and hormone production essential to a healthy mind and body. The more you know your personal circadian rhythm and what it takes to maintain it, the better you can control the depression that affects your sleep.

The Sleep Dilemma

As you've probably noticed, getting things done after a bad night's sleep can be extremely difficult even when you're not depressed. Trying to get on with your daily tasks when you're tired *and* depressed can be nearly impossible. Regulating your sleep schedule can directly affect your productivity in a positive way.

To find what works for you, you must first figure out which sleep problems are caused by depression and which ones are the product of work worries, relationship problems, or having too much to do. Examine what problems come and go depending on your mood. If you're normally a high-energy person and you suddenly see no point in getting out of bed or if you find you can't sleep at all due to tossing and turning, these might be signs that the sleep issues are depression-related. If your sleep problems are around even when your mood is more stable, these are the areas more under your control. Look to change those areas first.

Do you recognize any of these signs of depression-related sleep problems?

- You wake up too early and can't get back to sleep.
- You sleep more than usual.

- Your mind won't turn off when you get into bed.
- You sleep way more than is needed and still feel tired.
- You get into bed in the afternoon even though you had plenty of sleep the night before.

Jessica's Story

I have eight-year-old twins. When they have a slumber party, they are really noisy and never want to go to sleep. I try hard to remember that they're just little girls and this is normal, but on my down days, it just feels like too much.

I talked with my nurse practitioner about this and she had an amazing idea. She explained that all the light from the bright rooms and the DVDs the girls watch, along with the junk they eat, can cause a lot of pent-up energy. She suggested that one hour before bed, I turn off all the lights in the girls' room and light candles. The kids *love* this. I then heat some washcloths and sprinkle them with lavender oil. The kids lie on the floor and put the lavender-infused cloths over their faces. I tell them to just lie there and breathe in the great smell, and I do this, too. We are then in this fabulous low-light room filled with the scent of lavender. The girls' energy has completely changed by time we're done. I say, "Keep relaxed when you get into bed and talk in really low voices." I then read them a story and they fall asleep so much more easily. This helps me sleep a lot better as well.

My Story

When I'm depressed, I wake up around 4 in the morning and start to worry. All the things I know I should have done the day before and all the things I have to do that day start to swirl in my head. I worry about things much more than I need to. I go over conversations and have to deal with the stress of not having enough sleep. I'm not the type of person to sleep too much when I get depressed, but I do have trouble getting *enough* sleep.

What I do now:

- I know that staying out at karaoke past 11 P.M. will definitely affect my ability to get to sleep when I get home. I still do this sometimes, but I know the consequences and plan for them.

- When I travel to a different time zone, I get on the destination time one week before I go. This may mean going to bed at 9 P.M., but I do it. Otherwise, the jet lag can really cause depression for me.

- Since I've learned to get things done even when I'm depressed, I have less to worry about in terms of productivity when I go to sleep or wake up too early.

Exercise

It's essential that you figure out what, besides depression, adds to your sleep difficulties. Knowing that, you can then work to eliminate those troublemakers from your life so you can better work on the sleep problems actually caused by depression.

Check off the potential sleep disturbers in your life:

☐ Arguments about stressful events right before sleeping.

☐ Children's needs.

☐ More than 250 milligrams caffeine a day.*

☐ Smoking marijuana or having a drink before bed. (This promotes depression by interfering with deep sleep.)

☐ Worries about money and work.

☐ No set sleep hours.

☐ Medication problems.

☐ Nonconsistent shift work that changes your sleep schedule.

More than 250 milligrams caffeine a day has been shown to affect sleep. A regular 6-ounce cup of coffee has 125 milligrams. A decaffeinated coffee has 5 milligrams, and a cola can have 40 to 60 milligrams. A 6-ounce cup of black tea has 50 milligrams caffeine; the same amount of green tea has 30. Less than 250 milligrams caffeine a day is optimal.

Add yours here:

☐ _____

☐ _____

☐ _____

Ask yourself: *What can I do to reduce and end the things that seriously affect my ability to get a good night's sleep? How will making these changes affect my depression and my ability to get things done? What can I change immediately?*

ASK DR. PRESTON

Q Why do people with depression either sleep too much or too little? What's happening in the brain that causes so many sleep problems for depressed people?

A The hormone cortisol and a brain peptide (CRF or cortico-trophin releasing factor) are both released in higher amounts during times of depression. Both interfere with the depressed person's ability to go into slow wave or deep sleep. So whether or not a person experiences insomnia or even hypersomnia (sleeping way too much), they still experience chronic deprivation of deep, restorative sleep. In addition, it's common that people with depression have trouble with frequent awakenings at night and/or early morning awakening when they haven't had enough sleep.

Regulated Sleep Is Essential

It can't be stressed enough that good, regular, deep sleep is essential for a stable mood. It's also a requirement for maximum productivity. Your brain chemicals change during sleep in order to support your mood and physical body throughout your waking hours. Regular sleep gives you the energy you need to face the day and get things done, even if you feel depressed.

Here are the top five tips for restful sleep:

1. Get some regular exercise at least three hours before bed. Avoid exercising too close to bedtime.

2. Avoid substances that hold off or otherwise negatively affect deep sleep such as caffeine, alcohol, and overuse of tranquilizers.

3. Avoid taking unneeded naps, and be sure to wake up at the same time each day, even on the weekends. When you wake up, go outside for 10 minutes. (This regular exposure to outdoor light, even on a cloudy day, helps normalize your circadian rhythm.)

4. Keep your sleeping environment cool. A cooler body temperature enables you to go into deeper stages of sleep.

5. Check any medications you're taking for possible sleep side effects. Many antidepressants can affect sleep significantly.

Remember: If you do one thing when you put down this book today, think of your plan to get a good night's sleep. What do you need to do now?

Work with a Friend

When you're depressed, feelings of motivation, excitement, and the ability to work in a timely manner are often nonexistent. Yet you still have deadlines and obligations to meet. You might feel very alone and overwhelmed when you think of all you have to get done. This can be quite a detriment to getting going, especially in the morning.

Trying to take care of this alone can be very difficult. That's what friends are for, as the song goes.

Feed Off the Energy of Others

It can help to work with a friend who *does* have the energy, excitement, and productivity you lack. Maybe you have a positive friend who wants to help you but doesn't really know how. Now's the time to ask him or her to work with you on a specific project. Another person's positive energy can help immensely when you're down.

It's best if you work on a plan with a friend when you're not depressed so your friend can take action when you start to have trouble. A friend can help you set time limits that feel impossible to stick to when you're depressed. A friend can offer hope when you have none. Most importantly, a friend can help you become more productive when getting things done feels impossible.

Consider these benefits of working with a friend:

- You feel a lot less lonely.

- Your friend can help you manage your time more effectively.

- A nondepressed friend can help you get to places on time and stay as long as you need to.

- Collaboration creates positive energy, even if you work on separate projects. This is especially true if your friend is a co-worker.

Friends often want to help but aren't sure what to do. When you ask them for something specific, they can feel that they're making a difference in your life.

Lisa's Story

I'm a teacher, and I often have to write lesson plans. It's rotten to try to do this on a depressed day. I have a fellow teacher I really like, and we sit down and do our work together. She's not depressed, so I follow her example and work as hard as she does. It helps that I have to be there because we made a time to meet with each other. We go to a coffee shop that has big tables. I put on my headphones and feel so much better just seeing her across from me. I model her behavior, and my lesson plans get finished without such a terrible struggle.

My Story

I simply hate writing alone when I'm depressed. It's a necessary evil, of course, but I don't like it. I have trouble getting started and often leave my work space early due to lack of mental and physical comfort. When I leave early, I actually get more depressed because I know I'm not meeting my obligations. I often just wander around anyway. I'm so easily distracted when I don't have anybody to account to. I know this about myself and I'm finally learning to accept it. I need supervision! I need to know that I have to be somewhere at a certain time because someone else is depending on me.

What I do now:

- I have a friend who takes a class at the university where I write. She comes to see me after her class, and we have lunch. If I get to the library on time and work the four hours I want to, I know I get the reward of seeing her at the end of the work. I get my writing done a lot more easily as well. It especially helps if we study together.

- I've found that going to a coffee shop with a friend who also needs to get something done really makes a difference in my productivity.

- Just being out with people and watching someone else work triggers my ability to work.

- When I have to get certain tasks done such as cleaning my house, I have people in my life who are willing to do them with me.

- I make sure the person I meet is very disciplined and will hold me to our time together.

Exercise

What projects do you need to finish, and who can you work with to finish them? Look at the following examples and think of who you could work with:

Cleaning my house: mother

Hanging pictures: sister-in-law

Writing: roommate

E-mail: anyone who can just sit with me and do their own work

Paying bills: business partner

Finishing a work project: co-worker who has the same goals

You get the idea. Think of your projects and who you can work with to get them done.

Project   **Person**

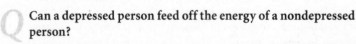

ASK DR. PRESTON

Q **Can a depressed person feed off the energy of a nondepressed person?**

A You'll have more success getting started and finishing projects when you're depressed if you have a buddy or coach to check in with. For example, let your wife know in the morning what you plan to do that day and then talk about it together that night. Working with a friend helps keep you focused on a project or conversation, and that helps keep you from focusing on your negative self-talk. Plus, human contact has always been shown to promote better physical and emotional health. What's more, energy begets energy, and just moving generates increases in serotonin levels and an improved mood.

Go Easy on Yourself

There's no reason to go it alone when you're depressed. Just taking the first step of talking with a friend about what you need can immediately improve your mood. Your friends and loved ones care about you and want to see you succeed. Use their energy to get started and keep going, even when you feel you don't have the energy to do anything.

For example, here are some suggestions for effectively working with a friend:

Have your friend drop you off and pick you up from a work location. This can be a very successful tool for those who have a hard time focusing and are easily distracted while working. Depending on the kind of work you have to do, not being able to leave can be a real impetus for you to work. Getting a friend to drop you off often works because you know when the person will be back and how long you have to work.

Have a friendly co-worker keep you motivated. Some people respond very well to orders from others and aggressive deadlines. These are the people who find it difficult to work alone or set their own schedule. If you're one of these people, finding a way to get a work friend to set your schedule and hold you to it may help. There's nothing wrong with being a more passive person when it comes to tasks. Not everyone can jump in and take charge. You may need incentive and hand-holding. A co-worker can do this if you're very clear on what you need.

Put yourself in a collaborative situation. Working with a group of friends can significantly increase your chances of finishing projects. This is one reason why study groups at school are so effective. If you're a mother or father with young children, join a play group. If you want to exercise more, join a team. This can certainly be hard when you're down and don't want to be with people, but you have to do it! You might not know anyone in the group when you start, but there's a good chance you'll make new friends while they help you get things done.

Find an organized friend to help you manage your bills. Paying bills can be one of the most difficult tasks you face when you're depressed. So many feelings can come up when you have to deal with money, and the actual logistics of the work can feel very overwhelming. This is when you can throw all your bills in a folder along with stamps, envelopes, and a checkbook and meet a friend for coffee. He or she can open the file, put things in piles, and hand you one item at a time to deal with. Maybe you can also ask a friend to help you set up automatic bill payments online.

Remember: The energy and expectations of a nondepressed friend are very powerful. You can tap into this energy when you work together.

Break Projects into Steps

One of the most common symptoms of depression is feeling overwhelmed when you're faced with large projects. It's as though you lose the ability to think, *Ah. A big project. What is my first step?* Instead, you think, *There's no way I can get* all *of this done!* When you combine this with the weariness and self-incrimination that often come with depression, the big stuff *can* be impossible because you may never even get started.

Think in Steps

When you get ready for bed at night, you perform certain steps. You brush your teeth after dinner. You may have a book near your bed or a CD you listen to. You turn off the light after you get into bed. You rarely do these out of order, and the steps make the night ritual a lot easier. You could say you have a recipe with specific steps for how to get into bed and to sleep with ease.

On the days when your work feels like a mountain you have to climb, you have to recognize that depression is making you feel this way and you *can* get past it. You can say to yourself, *I only have to do the steps in order and in a timely manner.* This will get you started.

There are many reasons why you may be overwhelmed by a project, including the following:

- You focus on an *entire* project instead of the steps.
- You don't know how to get started because you have no idea what to do first.
- You can't seem to get a handle on what needs to be done.
- You assume that something will have a lot more work and take a lot more time than it actually will.

When you break a project into steps, you at least know what to do first!

Rebecca's Story

I love to sew; it's something I've always enjoyed. On my good days, I just sew and it's no big deal. But for some reason, when I'm depressed, just getting out my machine is too much for me. I look at the pattern and it looks like an indecipherable plan. All I see are lines and geometric shapes. Then I think, *Making this skirt is so much work!* When I think of sewing as one big blob of work, I get overwhelmed and don't even get my machine out. Depression wins again!

When I started to deal with my depression in a different way, I simply said no to the overwhelmed feeling and reminded myself that I wanted to sew. I just had to take the time to rationally think of the steps involved. This isn't easy when I'm depressed, but I know that sewing makes me feel better. I tell myself, *One step at a time and then you go to the next one.* It sounds so simple, but doing this when I'm depressed really helps.

My Story

If I'd sat down and thought of this book as one big project, there's no way I would have finished. You're holding this book because I broke every single step into numbers and did them as separate projects:

(1) This book required 222 manuscript pages with 1-inch margins, single-spaced so I had to plan out how much room I had to write before I started the project. (2) I had to use a special font and required symbols to indicate where there were bullets and numbered lists. (3) I created an outline that needed to be used in each chapter. (4) I wrote out a detailed table of contents before I was even sure of what I wanted to say in detail. (5) I created 50 strategies for getting things done, and each one had to be three to five manuscript pages. (6) I carefully thought of how much space I would have left for the introduction. (7) I constantly reminded myself to be as creative as possible so you, the reader, wouldn't be bored while reading. (8) I made sure my ideas were clear and that I included a helpful exercise in each strategy. (9) I kept my writing at a very high standard, as my publisher is a big publishing company. (10) I sent my work to my friends and family for editing and then edited the chapters myself. (11) I organized a photo shoot with Dr. Preston. (The picture is on the back of the book!) (12) I delivered all of this on a very specific date even though I was often

depressed. (13) And finally, I did a final edit based on the suggestions of my editors.

What I do now:

- I work even when I'm depressed. It's slower and definitely more frustrating, but if I can say, *I'm doing step 5 today,* then I have a goal that's easier to complete.

- I get out a big piece of paper and my colored pens and outline everything before I get started. I then break down all the things I have to do into steps. This process can feel overwhelming, but I know it's an essential first step for all of my projects and that I'll be able to focus a *lot* better on what I have to do when I can see the steps first.

Exercise

No one, especially a beginning cook, would ever sit down and decide to bake a chocolate cake from scratch without a recipe that clearly showed the steps of the project. To get things done, just like that beginning cook, you have to have a recipe for all your complicated projects. Let's look at an example:

The "Applying for Graduate School" Recipe:

1. Research and decide on the schools that look best to you.

2. Look over the requirements you need to fulfill to send your application by highlighting them in the catalogue:

   - GRE or other test
   - Personal essay
   - Letters of recommendation
   - Transcripts
   - Application fee
   - Printing and copying

3. Go to the post office and send the application.

Now it's your turn. Pick a project that's really difficult when you're depressed such as cleaning your desk at work, washing and then changing the oil in your car, doing your bills, etc. Write your recipe steps here.

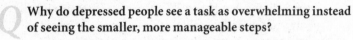

1. _____
2. _____
3. _____

It really makes a difference if you simply do one step at a time. Start with 1, do 2, and so on.

ASK DR. PRESTON

Q **Why do depressed people see a task as overwhelming instead of seeing the smaller, more manageable steps?**

A During depression, the mind starts to develop tunnel vision to mostly negative things. Some depressed people can also become very rigid in their thinking. They have trouble exploring creative alternatives to getting things done and instead listen to the voice that says there's only one way to do things. Finally, pessimism and a loss of self-confidence lead to predictions that what they decide to do will ultimately fail. To combat this, focus on small, simplistic, or concrete steps you can do fairly quickly. Your success will keep you moving.

Steps Work!

If you tried to do your task all at once, whether it was learning an acting role in one sitting or trying to speak a language before you've studied the grammar, there's a very good chance you'd get anxious, overwhelmed, and more depressed. You don't want that. You want to get things done, step by step. You can train yourself to look at every project like a recipe and know that you have many steps to go through before you get a beautiful and delicious cake—or an acting role or a second language.

Here are some other thoughts to consider:

- When you feel overwhelmed, write out the steps you need to take and include the time you think each task will take. You'll find that things usually take a lot less time than you estimated.

- Remind yourself that you are creative and you can find ways to work on a project, even if it feels overwhelming.

Remember: Everything feels impossible if you look at it as a whole instead of as a process with individual steps. In reality, the steps are all that matter, especially when you're depressed.

25

Ask Someone to Do the Little Stuff for You

Depression can make even the most mundane tasks feel impossible. It makes sense that doing a focused job at work when you're depressed would be difficult, but why is making dinner so hard? Why is it so difficult to hang up your clothes or get gas in the car?

Depression can take away your ability to do even the simplest of tasks. No matter how many strategies you use in this book, there will be some days when you simply can't get all the little stuff done.

It's Okay to Need Help

If you're usually able to do the little stuff with ease, it might be a shock to see how depression can totally take away this ability. You might start to feel like a burden if you can't fulfill your normal duties, and that can lead to the feeling that you're a failure simply because it's so hard for you to do the things others do with ease. This is when you need to ask the people in your life to take over and do the little stuff for you.

There's a difference between asking someone for help with a task, which implies a form of collaboration, and simply saying, "Please do this for me." Asking someone to actually do the stuff such as making a lunch, cleaning a room, or organizing a book shelf makes sense. If you simply aren't able to do what you have to do, getting someone else involved who can accomplish the tasks with ease is a good idea. Why put the added pressure of the little stuff on yourself when someone else can do it for you?

Look around you. Do you see any of the following signs that you would benefit from letting someone do the little stuff?

- Your office is unusable due to clutter.
- Your house is really dirty.
- You haven't cooked for a long time and you need a healthy meal.
- You cry at the thought of doing certain things.

Depression will tell you that this should all be easy! When you can tell it's not going to be easy at all, this is the time to ask for help.

Pat's Story

I have a 1969 Mustang that usually gives me a lot of pleasure. I've been restoring it for over a year. The engine is done, but the body needs a lot of work. When I got depressed last year after a layoff, my car no longer looked interesting to me. I didn't want to touch it. It seemed like an obstacle in my garage and only made me feel worse when I looked at it, as though it was saying, "Failure, failure, failure."

But there was a spark in me, even in the worst times, that said, *If you just go out there and do the work, you'll feel better.* My roommate would say, "God, Pat! Get out there and work on your car!" But I couldn't do it. This lasted for almost six months. My dad kept talking to me about it, but I blew him off.

Then one day I had an idea. I called my dad and said, "Would you come and take out the car and wash it, check the oil, and drive it?" He did. The car looked more friendly after that. He then started coming over once a week. For the next few months, we worked on the body together, and now I'm back to having fun with my car. I had to ask him to just do everything for me at first. I needed a model of "normal" behavior.

My Story

Depending on the seriousness of my depression, there are certain things I can and can't do in my life. When I get really depressed I stop cooking completely. It's just too much effort. I used to *really* get upset at myself about this. I've left clean dishes in the dishwasher for weeks now, even though I need to use them. I have clothes on the floor of my room. I have beautiful roses in my yard that I would love to have in my house, but I don't have the energy to cut them. This stuff happens when I'm quite depressed. I can take care of all this stuff when I'm moderately or mildly depressed, but there are just some times in my life when I need people to do things for me.

What I do now:

- I ask my brother to come and help me fix things around my house.

- I remind myself that needing this much help is not permanent.

- My mother knows what it means when I call and say, "I'm having a tough day." She knows that I probably feel over-whelmed with what I have to do around the house so she comes over and vacuums and cleans my kitchen.

- I talk to my friends and family about what I will sound like when I need them to do things for me. They know I will cry and feel embarrassed and guilty so they come over and take charge.

- I know only certain people in my life who can help in this way, and I make sure I don't overwhelm them.

Exercise

List five little tasks that are currently on your mind you need to get done but don't because you feel too depressed to do them. Then write who *can* do them.

The Little Nagging Tasks	Who Will Do Them?
_____	_____
_____	_____
_____	_____
_____	_____
_____	_____

Afraid to ask for help? Don't be; all you can get is a "no." And that's not rejection, just reality. You'll probably find that people will say yes because it makes them feel helpful and wanted. Just be honest. Say, "I can't do this. I need you to do this until it's done." When your mood is better, you can reciprocate.

ASK DR. PRESTON

Q **Why is it so hard to accept help from others when you're depressed?**

A Depression is a struggle against feeling completely powerless, so you might not ask for help because you don't want to feel like you're powerless or to appear that way to others.

And depression seems to reignite old emotional issues such as being shamed or remembering a "you need to stand on your own two feet" message from your parents. It might be that you hear an old message such as "you are incompetent," which could make it even more difficult to ask for help.

Asking for help might open an inner door that's full of sealed-off longings for others to take care of you. These longings can develop for many reasons. Many people had to grow up too fast and learn how to be autonomous before they were ready. Sometimes kids had to be a parent to their own parents. If you experienced this, it's normal that you would hold on to the "I'm completely self-reliant" persona. If that's the case, asking for help doesn't fit your self-image but may touch on deeply buried longings to be taken care of by someone else.

Or you might feel embarrassed to have others see your home or apartment because you haven't been able to keep it clean when you're depressed.

It's Okay to Ask

Asking for help and letting others help you with the small things is a positive and effective way for you to get the space and time you need to do the big things. There's no reason you have to do *everything*. When you're depressed, it's often the everyday things that get in your way. When you ask someone to do these small things, you can feel better knowing that they aren't hanging over you and pointing out what feels like failure.

Here are some ways to ask for help:

- "I'm so depressed today that the kitchen can't get clean. Would you do my kitchen?"
- "I've had trouble getting my CDs in order. They're all over the floor. Would you organize them for me?"
- "I can't get the kids to school. Would you please drive them?"
- "This part of the project is too much for me right now. Would you do it?"

When you're feeling better, you can return the favor.

Remember: The people who care about you want to help you. When you're too depressed to get things done, swallow your pride and ask them to do what you can't.

Learn to Say No

A *non*depressed person might take on too much and get stressed and overwhelmed if they say yes too often. As a person with depression, saying yes can have even more serious consequences. For one thing, saying yes when you need to say no is a surefire way to increase your depression. And not only will you have added to your workload, but you might also get down on yourself for not being strong enough to say no when you're asked to do something you don't want to do.

You *Can* Say No

Depression is not very nice. It either says you don't do enough or that what you do is no good. This can lead to a lot of saying yes on your part in order to please others. Depression can also take away your reasoning ability. When you're depressed, you probably have trouble asking, *Do I have the time and energy to do this project?*

Think of saying no more often. At first you might feel a lot of guilt as soon as you say no. Often the worry of how others react can increase this guilt. When you're depressed and you say yes due to the pressure from others or simply out of habit, you add more stress to your life. This basically guarantees that your down mood will last longer than if you had honored your own needs.

Read the following dialogue. If it sounds like you, you need to learn how to say no.

Michael's Story

Betsy and Michael meet in the hall of their small advertising firm:

Betsy: Hi, Michael. Do you have a minute? It's time for the holiday party. You're so great at planning things, and I loved what you did last year! It would be great if you would take care of the food again.

While Betsy is talking, Michael remembers that for the past two years, "taking care" of the food required an enormous amount of work. He missed out on the fun and felt resentful and unhappy the entire time because people kept coming up to him for help—"I ordered a vegetarian meal but I got chicken," etc.

Michael: Thanks, Betsy, but I really don't think I can do that this year. I'm sure someone else would like to do it. (*He's being his nice, normal, meek self. He doesn't want to make waves.*)

Betsy: I've asked people and they keep saying they loved what you did and that you should do it again! (*Obviously the people Betsy talked to know how to say no.*)

Michael: It was a lot of work last year, and I felt a bit over-whelmed. I have a lot to do in the office this week. A client is expecting something by next Friday. (*He's still giving her a way to convince him he can do his work and help out as well.*)

Betsy: Oh, come on, Mike, you did a great job! I promise I'll be there to help you. It's just the food. Other people are doing the games and stuff. It's going to be less stuff this year.

Michael: (*Feeling very pressured and guilty. He can hear a voice in his head say,* Just do it, Michael. Why do you worry about things so much?) All right, how many people will be there?

My Story

A friend of mine asked me to make jewelry for her wedding last summer. She offered to pay and made it clear it was fine for me to say no. Of course I said yes. Then she came over to describe what she wanted and that it was for six people! I started to feel resent-ment. Once I got started, I hated every minute of making that jewelry. I said to myself, *What were you thinking? People are always taking advantage of you. This is a waste of your time. It's ridiculous how you let people walk on you.*

Of course, this was all untrue. She by no means walked on me. She offered to pay. I'm the one who said, "Oh, don't worry, just pay for my supplies!" Dumb! I remember sitting there with my silver chain and crystals just seething. The stress started to get to me, and I got really negative every time I looked at my work. And it was all because I didn't really think about things and say no.

What I do now:

- I say no all the time.

- I force myself to say, "Let me think about that and get back to you." This isn't my personality, so it's really hard.

- I think of how saying yes will affect my mood before, during, and after the project.

- I ask myself if the project will get in the way of my own work.

- Sometimes when I say yes when I mean to say no, I have to make myself go back to the person and say, "I take back my yes. I meant to say no!"

Exercise

List five things you can say no to right now. Write down the thoughts that will come up with these decisions and then the way you will say no to the request. Here's an example:

Situation: A co-worker wants me to play a round of golf with his client on my day off.

Thoughts: This is one of my closest friends. How can I let him down? I have to say yes for our business as well. But I just don't feel up to it this weekend. I need time to myself. My work has been suffering lately because I've been so down. I'm finally feeling better, and I need to catch up.

How I can say no: "I understand that you want me to do this. Normally I'd say yes, but I have to get work done this weekend. I feel behind. I'll take a rain check."

Now it's your turn:

Situation: _____

_____

Why I want and need to say no: _____

_____

How I will say it: _____

_____

Feelings and thoughts that will come up and what I can do about them:

_____

_____

Ask Dr. Preston

Q **Why do depressed people have trouble saying no, sticking up for themselves, or knowing what they can realistically do in order to take care of themselves?**

A Thinking in complex ways is harder to do when a person is depressed. In other words, making choices, even relatively simple ones like where to eat out, can feel overwhelming. So they just say yes and then dislike their choice. Plus, low self-esteem leaves the person with feelings of self-doubt. This means a person says yes to get the situation resolved. The problem is that they don't focus on the consequences of the yes.

Tips for Saying No

Do you say yes all the time to please people? Or maybe it just feels easier to say yes and get the person to leave you alone. Does your family make you feel guilty when you say no? Are you of the martyr persuasion? No matter what the cause, you have to say no if you want to get your own things done when you're depressed. You owe it to your health and your productivity.

Let's look at how Michael says no:

Betsy and Michael meet in the hall.

Betsy: I've put you down for the food position. You are so great at planning things. The office party is going to be really fun this year. It would be great if you would take care of the food like you did last year. You did a great job.

Michael: Thanks for the offer. I've decided to just enjoy the party this year. I'm sure there's someone who likes to do this kind of thing.

Betsy: I've asked people and they keep saying that they loved what you did and that you should do it again!

Michael: Thanks for the compliment! People are so nice. (*He turns just enough so that she can see he is about to walk away.*) It's so great that you're putting this together this year. I think it will be a lot of fun. (*And he's out the door!*)

That's one way to say no. Here are some others:

- *Can you …?* No, I'm sorry I can't. *But …* That's my decision. Thanks for asking.

- *Can you …?* No, I'm sorry, I don't have the time for that. *But you're letting everyone down!* I'm sorry about that. I need to take care of myself right now.
- That's nice of you to suggest that, but no.
- No thank you.
- I don't think that will work for me right now.

Remember: It's easier to take a few minutes to say no than it is to worry over, obsess over, and then get depressed because of a yes you didn't want to say. Practice: *No thank you. No, that's nice of you. No, I can't. No, no, no, and again … no.*

Focus, Focus, Focus

When you're faced with a cloudy, depressed mind, you can drive around in circles, change your work location from one place to the next, forget where your kids are, miss work deadlines, and have trouble deciding what order to do things in. The projects you're supposed to do whirl around in your head like a swarm of bees, and somehow you're supposed to pluck one of them out of the swarm and get it done. This can feel pretty impossible if the tasks are so jumbled together you can't even think of all you have to do, much less what has to be done first.

Make Yourself Focus

This focus issue can seem so impossible to deal with, especially when you're late for a presentation, have to study for a test, or need to prepare an event. You can run around like a chicken for quite a long time without getting anything started. This happens because you lack focus. The good news is that you can *make* yourself focus when your brain can't.

Focus *is* a skill you can learn. It's a forceful way you can take over a situation when your thoughts are very unclear. It may be that your depression is mild on the days you can't focus. On these days, it's not that you lack desire for action. In fact, you do have the energy to get things done; you just don't have the precision it takes to really use your abilities. This is where forced focus can really help. When your depression is more serious, you have to work on focusing minute by minute. But it can be done.

Do you experience any of these signs of trouble focusing?

- Your head feels like a piece of cotton.
- You can't multitask.
- You float through the day.
- Your driving is very scattered and possibly dangerous.
- People have to talk to you a few times to get your attention.
- You have things to do, but you can't put them in order, so nothing gets done!

Focusing is hard enough when you're well. It takes practice to focus when you're depressed, but it's definitely possible.

Peter's Story

I run marathons. The running really, really helps my mood, but I've found that the athletic mentality I need is often lost when my mood is low. I have honestly run in circles a few times because I forget which way to go. Instead of focusing on my stride and how much water I need, my mind goes off on a tangent and I just run aimlessly.

This is different from getting into the zone. In fact, the zone is very, very focused. I can see everything clearly, hear my breath, remember my running form, and run with ease when I'm in the zone. It's harder to get into the zone when I'm depressed. I get around this by snapping myself back into my running by saying, "Run the right way, Peter! Get in stride. Focus on your feet and your form. What are your arms doing? Where are you going? What mile are you on? Where is your focus?" Not focusing when you run is dangerous; that's when injuries happen. When I run, I make sure I pull myself back into reality.

My Story

I woke up mildly depressed the other day. I felt a little relief from the more serious depression of the day before and decided I had a lot of things to get done. I got in my car and started driving. I then realized I had no idea where I was going. Should I go see my friend to get the clothes she got for me at a garage sale? Should I do the right thing and work on this book at the library? Should I go see my nephew, talk with my mother in her garden, call and schedule a trip I'm taking in a few weeks? Call my physical therapist? My goodness! It was like being in a dryer full of clothes. The options just went around and around.

What I do now:

* When I'm driving aimlessly with the brain fog, I yell at myself. *"Julie! Listen to me! Focus! Pull over and focus!!!"* (I talk to myself out loud a lot. It helps.) So I pull my car over and figure out what to do. I do have to stop my car or the driving is too distracting.

- I've found that making a decision on these days is not necessarily difficult. The problem is that I can't even focus on what needs to be done to make a decision. When I focus, the decision is a lot easier.

- When I'm working on a book, I find myself thinking about coffee or lunch, looking out the window, listening to the people around me, and basically letting my mind go on a mini vacation. But that doesn't get books written. I snap my head back to my computer and *focus!*

- I have to get things done in order to move forward with my career. If I sit down to do it, I might as well focus and do it right. Otherwise, it'll take double the time.

Exercise

You can teach yourself to focus. Imagine that your brain is a train on a track. When it gets off the track and starts to fall into a river, just focus and get it back on track! Look over the following situations and check the ideas that will work for you.

You have a lot of reading to do for a class and can't seem to concentrate. What do you do?

- ☐ Go somewhere quiet.
- ☐ Take a fast walk and then study.
- ☐ Study with a friend.
- ☐ Snap your mind back to the work when it wanders by saying "*Focus!*"
- ☐ Time what you do in small parts and focus on that small part only.
- ☐ _____

You're in a meeting and all you can think about is how miserable you are. What do you do?

- ☐ Look around you. Breathe and tell yourself, *I'm committed to listening to this meeting.*
- ☐ Take notes on everything that's being said so your mind is occupied.

☐   Sit up straight. Tighten all your muscles. Feel yourself sitting in the chair. Widen your eyes as much as you can, and let your body focus your mind.

☐   _____

Think of a time or task when you always have trouble focusing, such as following a map, reading meeting notes, answering e-mails, or cooking dinner. What can you do to focus the next time the situation comes up? Make a list you can use the next time your brain just won't cooperate with your need to get things done:

_____

_____

_____

_____

_____

ASK DR. PRESTON

Q   **Why does it help to yell "*Focus!*" out loud to yourself when you have a day where you can't focus? Does the brain hear it differently when you yell out loud?**

A   There's something about speaking out loud that helps you focus on the moment. Inner thoughts are likely to ramble and move in a negative direction. It's harder to think realistically under these conditions. Speaking out loud actually helps you do a better job of critical thinking so you can more easily spot distortions. Saying "Focus!" when you're in the middle of a hazy situation snaps you back into reality so you can do what needs to get done.

Similar help is found when you write down your thoughts. It elevates you into more conscious awareness and helps you view and carefully examine the situation to see if your conclusions or predictions are realistic and accurate.

Take Charge of Your Brain

Focus is possible when you're depressed. When you force yourself to focus, it's like giving your brain a wake-up call to get it back in line. Picture your mind as a camera lens. When the image is blurry, you can turn the lens until things become clear and easy to see. Use whatever image works for you, and force yourself to focus! You will always feel better when you do.

Here are some other thoughts on how to encourage focusing:

- Get comfortable talking to yourself out loud and forcefully.
- Know that you may have to say "Focus!" a lot when you're on a specific project.
- Keep your eye on the prize. Keeping the end result in mind helps you get things done!
- If distractions are the problem, remove yourself briefly, make a decision, and then get your mind back on track so you can successfully work despite the distractions.

Remember: Focus and depression are opposites. Depression takes away your ability to focus. You have to take it back.

Get Ready the Night Before

It cannot be emphasized enough: planning and structure can regulate your depressed brain and increase your ability to meet your obligations. When you wait to do things in the morning when you don't have enough time or the inclination to prepare for the day, you might find that you not only increase your depression, but your level of anxiety can increase as well. This isn't a great way to start your day when you're already having trouble keeping a positive attitude.

Get Into the Groove

For many people, morning isn't the best time to take on big tasks. The evening can be much more productive. Take a half hour each night to get things ready for the next day: your clothes, lunch, directions to a new appointment, or anything that will make you feel rushed in the morning. Create an assembly line if you need to. Work from a checklist. Do anything and everything you can at night. It works.

Getting ready for your day the night before is a daily solution to a daily problem. This behavior can become a habit. When you make it your goal to roll out of bed fully prepared for the day, your mood can at least be more stable because you've eliminated the added stress that comes from rushing in the morning.

Consider the following signs that you need to prepare at night:

- You're very scattered and overwhelmed when you wake up.
- You're hard on yourself for not thinking ahead.
- You forget things and have to go back inside.
- Your organizational ability is lessened due to depression, and the morning is chaos.
- Your mood suffers for the rest of the morning.

It's normal if you want to relax at night after a long day, but it does make sense to take even 15 minutes to get ready for the morning.

Peter's Story

I'm a single father with three girls. I'm honest with them about my depression problems, and they want to help me. We decided that getting ready for the next day before we go to sleep makes the house run a lot more smoothly.

They're old enough to do a lot of chores on their own. My youngest is 11. She's responsible for getting her softball clothes and equipment ready, as well as her lunch. My middle daughter takes a long time in the bathroom in the morning. I've had a hard time getting her to follow a new nighttime plan, but when I tell her it's for me and not a punishment on her, things get better. My oldest daughter is a senior in high school. She does lunches for anyone who needs one and makes sure the dishes are washed so we don't wake up to a junky kitchen.

I set the timer on my coffeemaker the night before. The car has gas. They have their spending money ready. Any after-school stuff goes on the big calendar on the fridge, and we look at it the night before as a group. This may sound a bit regimented, especially for three girls, but they want to help me. I know for a fact that it makes their lives a lot easier as well. There's a lot less arguing in the morning for all of us.

My Story

I often wake up and feel rushed and worried. I realize that I've forgotten some things that I'll have to coordinate to meet the obligations of my day. I think, *Wait a minute! I work until 4, but I have to meet someone at 5? I can't wear the same clothes! I'll have to take something different with me.* Then I realize I have no lunch and not much food in the fridge. I recently went to a cash-only system and have to plan my money each day. If I wait until the morning to do this, I often forget all my money and have to borrow from friends. I find that I'm not really aware of how much time it takes to get ready. I'm known for getting out of my car and going back inside two to three times for things I've forgotten.

What I do now:

- If I have to go to a meeting the next day, for example, I have the directions printed out, the phone number of the person I have to meet, all of my paperwork, a pad for notes, gas in the car, and a breakfast ready.

- I get my mind ready the night before as well. I know I might wake up depressed, so I have a plan. I remind myself as I go to sleep that my day *will* have meaning and then I think of the things I'm going to do that day, so I can remember it all if I wake up with bad thoughts.

- I'm tired of getting halfway to where I need to go and having to turn back. Preparing ahead prevents this.

Exercise

Think of what you have to do tomorrow. What can you get ready tonight so tomorrow goes more smoothly? Do any of these examples apply?

- Take a shower before bed.
- Decide on breakfast and lay it out.
- Prepare lunch so you can just pick it up and go.
- Decide what money you will need.
- Get your clothes ready to wear and ironed, if necessary.
- Plan on where you need to be at certain hours.
- Be sure there's gas in the car.
- Check to see if your family needs something prepared for the morning.

List five things you usually don't have time to do in the morning:

1. _____
2. _____
3. _____
4. _____
5. _____

The list can get pretty long, but it's better to do these things the night before than to wait until you have less time and can be overwhelmed. Write out your plan and stick to it, even when you want to sit in front of the TV or take time for yourself at night. You can prepare ahead in as little as 15 minutes, but those few minutes can save you hours of stress the next day.

ASK DR. PRESTON

Why does it help to plan everything you need to do in a day the night before?

In large group studies, it's been found that most people with serious depression function worse first thing in the morning because of less energy, more pessimism, and trouble concentrating. The night before can be a much more productive time to plan out a schedule and get things done.

You Have More Time at Night

Many people have time limitations in the morning, especially if they have a tendency to oversleep. Your time and energy are often more available at night. After you take the short time of preparing ahead, you can have a better morning and a more relaxed evening as well.

Here are some other thoughts to consider:

- Get your kids to do all they can the night before.
- Choose two things to do in the morning such as taking a shower or playing with your dog, and do all the rest the night before.
- Be realistic about how much time you actually have in the morning and plan accordingly.
- Create a checklist each night of what you have to get done.
- Put all objects that will go with you into the car the night before.
- Check all appointments and decide what documents you have to take.

Remember: Depression makes it hard enough to get going in the morning. Why add to the problem by rushing around after your alarm rings?

Expect to Have Trouble Thinking

Depression is caused by faulty brain functioning. You might wonder, *Why is thinking so hard for me? What's wrong with me? My thinking is so slow. I've read this paragraph 15 times, and I still can't remember it. Am I just getting old?*

The thinking problems that lead to these questions are normal. No matter how smart you are or how proficient, there will be days when you can't find your car in a parking lot, paying bills will feel like doing calculus, and reading a map will feel impossible. This happens because your brain is not at its best.

Overriding a Confused Brain

Being depressed is like having a broken car. You turn on the windshield wipers, and instead the lights go on. When you turn on the lights, the radio starts playing. The cylinders aren't firing, and of course you will always leave your keys in the car! Memory problems due to depression can be intense and affect your work performance. You can have problems so severe that your doctor sends you in for attention-deficit hyperactivity disorder (ADHD) testing, and you might get an incorrect diagnosis.

The best way to deal with these problems is to accept that they are going to happen. Your brain is not deteriorating, and you're not "getting old." These thinking problems will come and go when they're a product of depression. That means you have to be more diligent with your work and go easier on yourself.

Do you recognize any of these signs indicating you're having trouble thinking?

- Lack of focus
- Poor memory
- Being easily distracted
- Trouble retaining information

A depressed brain is often a fuzzy brain. Expect it and find ways to work around it.

Roberto's Story

I have a fishing guide business. When I have a client, I have a lot of stuff to get ready. I also have to be very careful about safety or I could lose my license. I'm very aware of the days that are going to be tough. I have trouble using the ropes to tie up the boat and trailer, which is usually very easy for me. I think over and over again about what time the trip starts, and then worry I have the time wrong.

My trouble is organization. I have to do things in order with this work. I have to check the boat. I have to have all the poles, lures, life jackets, and a lot of other little things. I provide lunch, so I have to pack that. I then have to put the boat on the trailer and make sure it's safe. I feel like I'm doing all of this underwater when I'm scattered and down.

The first thing I do is focus on how the work always makes me feel better and then I go over a mental checklist, which straightens out my thoughts. I can do this even when my brain isn't thinking clearly. I can override the jumble. I specifically think of all I have to do regarding the boat, then the fishing gear, then the clients, then getting to the site. This breaks everything into chunks, which I can manage better.

My Story

I can't count the times I've lost my car in a parking lot or on the street. I walk outside to find the car and literally can't remember where I last saw it. I remember street names, but I'm not sure if the names are from today or the day before. I see cars that look like mine, but they aren't.

Then there's reading maps and trying to find a new location. I get my directions off the Internet and often have to read them four or five times while I'm driving. Even if I've gone to a house many times, I can't remember the exit and often have to ask for the address again. I get confused and anxious, and I certainly feel stupid. I forget appointments to the point that I double-book and then miss something important. I've lost a lot of money this way.

I have a day planner, but I often forget to look at it. This is not just ordinary forgetfulness. It's much worse when I'm depressed, especially if I'm anxious as well.

What I do now:

- When I get out of my car, I look for landmarks as well as the street name. I can often forget the street name, but not the restaurant I'm parked in front of.

- I tell people I can't remember names and that they'll have to remind me. And no, it's not "old age"!

- I accept that I can't remember numbers when I'm down. I have trouble counting money and feel overwhelmed by bills and simple math.

- I ask for reminder calls from all my appointments, if possible. Many of my friends call the day before we meet.

- My family and friends know they have to be patient with my thinking issues. They know those issues will go away when I feel better.

Exercise

When is your thinking at its worst—morning, afternoon, or night? What can you change so you don't have to do something at your least effective time?

_____

_____

_____

_____

_____

What part of your thinking does depression affect the most?

- ☐ Concentration   ☐ Memory
- ☐ Numbers   ☐ Reading
- ☐ Time management   ☐ Creativity
- ☐ Studying

When this happens, what are you going to do to increase your brain power?

- ☐ Make yourself get back on track by talking yourself through the project.
- ☐ Keep away from the analytical stuff until your brain is in better form.
- ☐ Stop and breathe.
- ☐ Imagine your brain engaging, and make it happen.

ASK DR. PRESTON

Q

Why does depression cause memory problems?

A

The main problem is that people are often preoccupied with inner thoughts and worries. If they can reduce these, their thinking skills can improve. Plus, it takes energy to keep themselves thinking clearly, and people with depression often lack this energy. Thinking problems can especially spiral out of control if people constantly think and talk about how they can't remember anything. This just perpetuates the problem by making them more frustrated.

Q

What's the difference between depression and ADHD?

A

People with ADHD have very distinctive symptoms: hyperactivity, poor ability to maintain sustained attention (especially to boring or tedious tasks), being easily distracted, difficulty planning ahead, and a tendency to act impulsively. With depression, a person might have difficulty concentrating, but it's due more to preoccupation with negative inner thinking and worries.

A second difference is in the neurobiology of the brain. With depression, there's marked decrease in brain activity in many different areas of the brain. This isn't the case with ADHD. With ADHD, there's a problem with the neurotransmitter dopamine. Dopamine activity in the frontal lobes is significantly reduced. All drugs that successfully treat ADHD work to increase dopamine activity. This is not the case with depression medications. So people with depression can have ADHD-style thinking problems while not technically having ADHD at all.

You Can Train Your Brain

It's very common for thinking problems to take over without your awareness, and your tasks can significantly suffer. Be aware of what it feels like when your brain is not operating optimally and go into strategy mode immediately.

Here are some other thoughts to consider:

- When you begin to have trouble thinking, stop what you're doing and stand still until you can make your brain work again. By slowing down, you can better engage the parts of your brain you need to do specific tasks.

- If you're working in a situation that requires extreme thinking skills and concentration, such as surgery or police work, you *must* anticipate the problem and ask yourself if you're capable of doing the job—before you're in the situation. If this problem persists for more than a few days, take a break from your work and see a mental health professional for help.

- If you're an older person, thinking problems may be associated with aging. In reality, many studies show that aging is by no means a guarantee of diminished thinking. Focus on what depression is doing instead of blaming it on your "aging brain cells."

Remember: Think of your mind as an old-style clicking watch. See it go through each rung. When the clicking gets stuck, you have to get the click back on track. Visualize it, and make your brain work optimally again.

Beware Caffeine and Sugar Highs

Ah, caffeine and sugar. For many people who are depressed, these can feel like a gift from heaven in an otherwise dark and dismal life. They can also create a sense of increased energy and an ease in getting started on projects. Unfortunately, many of these supposed benefits are illusions. Like many pleasurable things, the aftereffects are the problem, not the actual imbibing!

Why Caffeine and Sugar Affect Your Mood

Caffeine is a mind-altering substance that affects your brain chemicals and your body. Many people use caffeine as a treatment for depression. You might say, "It gives me energy when I'm depressed" or "I'm so tired when I wake up in the morning, I have to have coffee to get going!" But caffeine can significantly affect anxiety as well as your ability to get a good night's sleep, and the negative effects can by far outweigh the positive.

And then there's sugar. Mood fluctuations and energy levels are strongly impacted by the ups and downs of blood sugar levels. It's essential that you maintain even blood sugar levels in order to manage depression. When the sugar high from a pint of chocolate ice cream wears off, your blood sugar level dips and you want to get that high feeling back, so you eat more! You can probably see how this stresses your body and isn't exactly a great way to treat your mood. A donut and a soft drink might feel good at 4 P.M. when your energy lags, but an apple is a far better choice. Put some peanut butter on it and pretend it's a peanut butter cup!

Do you recognize any of these signs you use caffeine and sugar to treat depression?

- Your mood feels better at the first sip of coffee or soft drink.
- Your cravings for caffeine and sugary junk food increase when you're depressed.

- You're overweight from ice cream, cake, candy, and cookies.
- You have three mochas a day!
- Your mood and energy lag significantly in the afternoon.

It's natural that you'd want to use a substance that makes you feel better in the moment. When this happens, ask yourself how you will feel in three to four hours and go from there.

Brad's Story

I once felt really stressed at work. I was restoring an old building to make it look like its original interior, which meant a lot of woodwork. One day, I tried to fit a drawer into a desk and it wouldn't go. I was having a bad day already—depression makes me irritable and angry. When the drawer problem happened, I said out loud, "I need some candy!" and went straight to the convenience shop next door. I had peanut M&M's, ice cream, and a Snapple. When I went back to work, my painting partner laughed and laughed. He said, "I've heard a lot of people say 'I need a drink!' but you're the first person I've heard say 'I need candy!'"

He's right. I use candy to feel better. I don't have a weight problem at all. In fact, I have trouble keeping weight on due to my antidepressant. The candy makes me feel better. My mom keeps telling me to stop. I don't see myself replacing it with a banana or anything, but I do see that I crave it a lot more when I'm in an irritated, depressed mood. I know I need to cut down.

My Story

As I sit here writing, I'm thinking of the amazing iced coffee I can buy at a restaurant across the street. It's very, very bad for me. Unfortunately, it's the best iced coffee I've had in many years. It's made with a special cold-water process that creates a smooth and heavenly taste. The problem is that this method doubles the caffeine in a glass. I switched to decaf years ago. It tastes okay and doesn't affect me too strongly, but compared to that iced coffee, it's not exactly satisfying.

I have the caffeinated coffee once in a while. I then shake and get nervous for a few hours. If I have it on depressed or anxious days, I get so agitated I have trouble working. I have a friend who has anxiety problems, and it does the same thing to her. As you can tell, this coffee isn't in my best interests. I don't drink it for the energy; I just love the taste.

What I do now:

- I know that caffeine and my brain don't mix very well.

- I focus on what caffeine does in the long term instead of the short term.

- I drink decaffeinated coffee 90 percent of the time.

- I know the consequences if I drink the evil stuff!

- When I do get back into the dangerous cycle of eating sugar and drinking coffee, I work to get out of the cycle daily, especially considering that I can gain a lot of weight in a short amount of time. It will probably be a lifelong challenge, but what matters is that I keep going.

Exercise

How does caffeine affect you? Considering the pervasiveness of caffeine drinks in coffee shops on every corner, finding ways to get caffeine is easy. What isn't easy is admitting that the caffeine may be doing a lot more harm than you think. Look over the following statements and check the ones that are true for you:

- ☐ It gives me energy in the morning.
- ☐ I love the taste.
- ☐ It gives me something to do with friends.
- ☐ It's a lot better than having a martini every day!
- ☐ It's expensive.
- ☐ It's a habit.
- ☐ I don't really like coffee; I'm just physically addicted.
- ☐ I get headaches if I stop drinking it.
- ☐ It produces anxiety and shaking.
- ☐ A latte breaks up the monotony of my workday.
- ☐ It causes me to have trouble sleeping.
- ☐ I can't stop even though I promise myself I will.
- ☐ It doesn't really help my depression at all.

How does sugar affect you? It seems impossible these days to find products that *don't* contain sugar. It tastes good and it's inexpensive. Once again, it's a substance that tends to boost the mood for a short while and then you're back where you started. If you have weight problems due to sugar, it's especially important that you get honest and do something about it. Weight gain and poor nutrition not only affect your physical body, they can make you feel terrible about yourself, which is depressing enough! Look over the following statements and check off the ones that are true for you:

- ☐ Tastes so good!
- ☐ It's cheap.
- ☐ It's an easy high.
- ☐ There's no fat in it if I just eat gummy bears.
- ☐ Chocolate is good for me—I read it on the Internet!
- ☐ I need something to feel better when I'm depressed.
- ☐ It's something I can do when I'm alone.
- ☐ Milkshakes are a perfect food.
- ☐ It makes me fat.
- ☐ I can't stop eating it once I start.
- ☐ It calls to me from the kitchen.
- ☐ It tastes so good, I eat until I'm sick.
- ☐ I eat it instead of nutritious food.
- ☐ I hide, steal, and hoard it.
- ☐ I want to stop but can't imagine life without sugar.
- ☐ It doesn't really help my depression at all.

You're very smart regarding caffeine and sugar. Only you know if it's a normal, controlled, and positive part of your life or if it's an addicted, out-of-control, negative part of your life. What do you want to do if it is a problem?

_____

_____

_____

_____

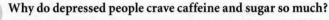

ASK DR. PRESTON

Q **Why do depressed people crave caffeine and sugar so much?**

A Sugar very transiently increases energy. In lab tests, it's been found that chocolate increases dopamine (the main "feel-good" neurotransmitter) in the brains of rats. Caffeine also has mood-elevating effects that are felt rapidly yet only last 15 to 20 minutes. In the long run, too much sugar or caffeine can increase depression, especially by sugar's effect on your blood sugar and by caffeine's negative impact on deep sleep.

It's Up to You

Caffeine and sugar consumption really are your choice. Only you know how to regulate what you put in your body. You're an adult. If you're using caffeine and sugar to feel better and it's not working in the long term, decide what's more important—your moods or fleeting energy and pleasure. Overconsuming caffeine and sugar can lead to so many problems—anxiety, shame, and sleep problems, to name a few. Think carefully before you put something in your body that's making you more depressed.

Here are some other thoughts to consider:

- If you're having agitated depression, the best thing you can do is to stop caffeine completely or switch to decaffeinated. It might be very hard, but increasing agitated depression is worse.

- If you feel immediately better when you eat sugar, you're probably dependent on that sugar emotionally and physically. The first step is awareness. When the craving starts and the sugar hits your body, ask yourself, *What just happened that made me crave this? Can I focus on that for a minute?*

- Try to limit your caffeine consumption to 250 milligrams or less per day, and only have it in the morning (to avoid interference with sleep). Decaffeinated coffee is an acquired taste, and you can get used to it. If you have more than 750 milligrams coffee a day (more than 5 cups), I suggest you cut down.

- Switch to tea. Even black tea has less caffeine than coffee, and you can get used to the taste and start to like it over time.

Remember: Many substances make you feel better in the moment, but those aren't always the best choice, considering the low they create when they leave your system only makes you need them more. That's how vicious cycles get started.

Distinguish Between Depression and Low Self-Esteem

It's easy to confuse depression with low self-esteem, considering that depression symptoms can mimic self-esteem issues. When you're depressed, it's normal to examine the past for answers as to why you're often down and can't work to your full potential. It's easy to blame your symptoms on your childhood or a lack of belief in yourself and your abilities. But it's very important to know the distinction between the two. Depression might seem like a self-esteem problem, but for many people this is not the case. Self-esteem issues rarely make it hard to get out of bed, clean a house, or wash a car.

Why Self-Help Books Might Not Work

Self-help books often prescribe emotional change. They're extremely helpful if they're used in the right situation, but the problem for the depressed person is that self-help books suggest *you* completely control your destiny and, thus, are the sole cause of your difficulties. The more change-oriented a book is, the easier it is to feel like a failure when feelings of self-worth don't respond positively to the suggestions offered.

Self-help books that emphasize action steps with an understanding of the physical causes of depression can be very effective, but it helps if you read any self-help book with a natural skepticism.

It's very important that you distinguish the problems directly related to your past from the problems created in the present by depression. There really is a great difference. And until you recognize the difference, you could spend many years looking for causes of your hopelessness, lack of belief in yourself, and an inability to get things done as something psychological when it was a physiological reason all along.

What's the difference between depression and low self-esteem?

- Self-esteem issues can often make sense; many times you can trace them to exact events such as an experience in your past or hating your body due to society's emphasis on a certain body type.

- Depression often goes further than low self-esteem—the language, self-punishment, crying, and inability to get things done are typically more severe.

- Self-esteem problems usually respond well to therapy sessions. Physically based depression often needs more medical and behavioral treatment than therapy alone.

American television shows, for example, can be very focused on changing patterns that cause life troubles. If you watch these shows, always think of what's the real you and what is the depressed you and go from there.

Martin's Story

I've always blamed my problems on my childhood. My lack of work ability was due to the fact that my father never taught me anything about business. My restlessness was due to our moving all of the time. My trouble in school was because my mother never did homework with me. The list was endless.

Looking back, I feel sad for my family. I really thought how I was raised was what made me such a "failure." I didn't notice that my brothers, raised in the exact same environment, didn't feel the same at all. And to be honest, my relationship with my parents wasn't bad; I just had to blame someone. I never, ever thought it could be depression, so I kept seeking help from books and anything else I could study. And still, I felt this nagging thought that someone had done me wrong!

When I was diagnosed with depression and finally started to get better, I couldn't believe what a different person I was. Completely different. Not only was I able to focus on the present instead of constantly thinking about the past, I was actually able to see my childhood for what it was: pretty normal.

My Story

I saw therapists for 20 years for what I thought were self-esteem issues. I couldn't figure out why I was always so down on myself and my lack of accomplishments, when in reality, I often accomplished just as much as the people in my life.

When I'm depressed, I feel that my relationship with my mother is terrible and that something she did in my childhood was responsible for my low self-esteem. When I'm well, I think nothing like this! I know for a fact that my mother has nothing to do with my depression. But when I'm sick, I always look to find out what I or others did wrong. Was I not encouraged as a child? Were my parents too harsh? Is the project just too hard for me? Do I just need to work on myself more?

What I do now:

- I know I have a physiological illness that affects my view of myself. I started to have a much better self-image when I looked at an outside cause—depression—instead of an internal self-esteem cause. I now know I'll have "low self-esteem" issues when I'm depressed and that they will usually go away when I get well. I'm used to it.

- I make sure that when I read self-help books, I can tell what will work for me and what won't. For example, if a book says, "Depression is simply a lack of hope, and if you truly look deeper in yourself and see your spiritual crisis, the depression can end," it makes me very, very angry. This shows a potentially dangerous lack of understanding of the real causes of my depression. But now, I realize many suggestions won't work for me and I keep treating the depression with my strategies. I know I don't have a deep spiritual problem.

Exercise

Look over the following list. What do you say and feel regarding getting things done?

- *My work is always subpar.*
- *I feel inadequate at work.*
- *I can't seem to get my act together.*
- *I've been a failure all my life.*
- *Romantic relationships are difficult for me.*
- *I'm so easily distracted.*

- *I'm such a boring person.*
- *I don't really know how to let someone love me.*
- *My body is ugly.*
- *People judge me because of my lack of education.*
- *I have trouble making and maintaining friends.*
- *Everyone else has more fun than I do.*
- *I don't enjoy my work.*

Then ask yourself the most important question: *Do I have these thoughts and issues as seriously when I'm not depressed? In fact, are some of these issues not issues at all when I'm not depressed?* If the answer is no, your "issues" are probably depression-related and can be successfully treated with depression management. If you regularly feel a majority of the items on the list and they only get worse with depression, therapy that explores your past and how it affects your worldview might be a good idea.

ASK DR. PRESTON

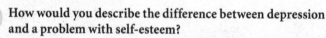

Q **How would you describe the difference between depression and a problem with self-esteem?**

A Depending on how you were treated in your family, you grew up with ideas about yourself and others that often reflect your upbringing. These deeply ingrained beliefs can be positive or negative. Positive beliefs such as *I'm basically a decent and likable person,* or *If I try hard enough, I am generally able to accomplish things, even if they're challenging* naturally lead to the belief in positive outcomes.

Negative beliefs include *I'm worthless* or *When people really get to know me, they'll see that I'm a loser and abandon me.* People with *chronically* low self-esteem live with these beliefs *every day.* The person with chronically low self-esteem *continuously* reads negative things into a multitude of life circumstances.

For some people with depression, dormant negative beliefs that have successfully been worked on in therapy or through self-growth work often get reactivated and *are only present during the depressive episode.* Others, even those with normally positive beliefs, can experience sudden negative beliefs that are shocking and make little sense considering life circumstances.

When assessing someone with depression, it's important to try to determine if the current low-self-esteem symptoms are episode-related and will end once the depression is treated successfully, or if they are long-standing traits that can be addressed with therapy.

Know the Difference

If you have problems with body image, relationships, work, and negative beliefs about yourself that are long term and stay pretty constant in your life, they might be due to low self-esteem. If you find that your life issues come and go or get a lot worse depending on your moods, you might find that these problems go away when your depression is managed successfully.

Here are some other thoughts to consider:

- Be very aware of what self-esteem-*style* symptoms come and go depending on your mood.

- Look deep inside and be honest with yourself about your lack of enthusiasm and ability to do what you want to do. Was this present when you were a kid? Did you learn it from a family member? Have you struggled with this forever and are not sure what to do? You might have low self-esteem, which can benefit from talk therapy.

Remember: Working on personal problems caused by the past is very important. Knowing when the problems are due to a malfunctioning brain is essential.

Avoid Isolation

One of the problems with depression is that the symptoms created by the illness are often cured by the opposite behavior. This is especially true with the isolation depression creates. Depression-induced isolation often leads to loneliness and the belief that you'll be this way forever, no matter how many people you have in your life.

Getting things done is not always a solitary process, and the more you isolate yourself, the less chance you have of finishing projects, especially those you need outside help with. Serious isolation can range from staying in bed all day to avoiding all your family and work obligations.

Being Alone Is Not Always a Good Thing

If depression makes you just want to go into a room and be left alone, you have to seriously think about how this is affecting your productive life. Just thinking can be difficult, but this is one of the strategies that's not really up for discussion when you have to get things done. Depression can be successfully treated by action and by being with other human beings.

The solution to the isolation caused by depression is being with people. This is one of the most difficult strategies you'll need to use to get better, but it will help you get out of the depression-seclusion cell and become a productive part of the world again.

Are any of these signs of "hermit" behavior familiar to you?

- You can't find the words to talk with other people.
- You cancel events that once gave you pleasure.
- Your work suffers because you can't work with others.
- You don't leave your house.
- You really do think it's better to just be alone and deal with depression yourself.
- You're very, very lonely, yet find it difficult to be with people.

If you want to be by yourself when you're depressed, ask yourself why. If the answer is that it recharges you so you can go back into the world, the time alone is effective. If otherwise, ask yourself what will make you feel better, being alone or getting out and taking part in life?

Maxim's Story

I stayed in my room for a week once. I don't want to go back to that kind of behavior. I didn't answer the phone, and when I did talk to people, I told them I just needed to be alone to think. It was the lowest time of my life. I didn't eat and drank a lot of beer. I honestly didn't know what was wrong. It's like I was in a daze and couldn't get out of it.

One day I woke up and the real me said, *Enough! Get out of this house!* I'm not sure where the voice came from, but it worked. What a waste of my life. I saw a doctor after that and started on an antidepressant. I also got a roommate, which helped a lot. I doubt I would stay in my house for a week if someone knew what was going on. I'm lucky that I kept my job because I lied that I had the flu. Now I'm honest, and if I have a rough day, my roommate gets me out of the house.

My Story

Why does depression make me feel so unbelievably lonely? I think about this a lot. Working alone makes this even worse. I long for an office setting where I can talk to people in the hall and go into people's offices and just say hi. I know many people would love to be home and not have to go to an office, but being alone is hard for me when my brain is sick. I've cried many nights over this feeling. I start to plan how I can work with people and be with people and stop being alone so much, and this helps me move out of the loneliness.

What I do now:

- I know that living alone doesn't work for me at all. It makes me a lot more depressed. I always live with someone now.

- I remind myself that being alone is not an indication that I'm alone in life. There's a big difference. Being alone is a natural part of life, and I have to learn to deal with it.

- Writing is lonely work sometimes. That's just a fact. I do what I can to get the work done so I can go see people. And I have to be realistic and remember that I'm really only alone when I write.

- I pack my days full with things to do. As an extrovert, I thrive on this. When I'm depressed, it's essential. This means the hours of alone time when I write have a time limit.

Exercise

Set up an isolation action plan before you get too depressed to see other people. Look over the following section and start to create your own plan for the days when you just want to be alone but you know it would be much better for your depression to get out and be with people.

☐ Make myself presentable every single day.

☐ Always go to work.

☐ Plan something I can't get out of.

☐ Ask the people in my life to *make* me get out.

☐ Think of how I will feel after I do something.

☐ Just do the first step.

☐ Remember what I loved in the past and do it now.

Yes, ending isolation is one of the most difficult strategies in this book. But it's also one of the most important. Look at the preceding list and then write five things you can do to end isolation in order of their ease—and then do the first one right now!

1. _____

2. _____

3. _____

4. _____

5. _____

ASK DR. PRESTON

Why is depression so isolating?

When you're depressed, it's natural if you want to pull away from others. You learn early on when dealing with depression that many friends or family members don't want to hear you complain or in other ways express your negative feelings. Often you conclude, *No one wants to be around me ...* and, thus, you seclude yourself. This conclusion can be based in part on the actual fact that people *don't* want to be around you when you're depressed, but it can also be due to the feelings of low self-esteem depression can create.

Others who are depressed conclude that they won't have much to say. Like a preemptive strike, rather than risk being rejected, you choose isolation. And the combination of low energy, low motivation, and the overly negative prediction that to be with others will be unpleasant also contributes. This is classic depressive thinking.

Isolation—although it may be very understandable during a depressive episode—is one of the worst things a depressed person can do. It's a symptom that fuels the fires of depression. Studies have shown convincingly that treatments for depression that solely focus on keeping people engaged with others can reduce depression significantly.

Just Do One Thing

Make it a goal right now that you will get out and be with people. You might just sit there and watch others. You might not participate. You might watch people throw a Frisbee, work on a project, go to the movies, or do volunteer work. That's okay. Let others give you energy. Let others help you feel better! It often only takes one time and you can start to feel more connected. When you realize that being with others is better than being cut off, you'll have more energy and productivity.

Here are some other thoughts to consider:

- Decide that isolation is not an option, no matter how you feel. Make it a goal to get outside your house and at least walk around people one hour every day.

- Remind yourself constantly that you're a person worthy of human contact.

- If you love animals, find a way to be around animals and then transfer that energy to people.

- Go to work and/or school with no room for negotiation with your brain.

Remember: Depression is isolating. Reach out. You'll always feel better. Always.

Always Do Your Best

Don Miguel Ruiz, in his book *The Four Agreements,* says: "Your best is going to change from moment to moment; it will be different when you're healthy as opposed to sick. Under any circumstance, simply do your best, and you will avoid self judgment, self abuse and regret." Depression doesn't actually let you have this kind of realistic thinking, does it?! When you're depressed, your best probably won't be your normal "best." The only way around this is to do what you can to the best of your ability and then be really proud of yourself for getting *something* done.

Your Best Will Change

For most people, depression limits their ability to work productively when compared to their nondepressed times. For some, their productivity is severely limited. For others, it might be periodic. No matter where you fall on the spectrum, the only way to make it through the tough times is to do your best. If you think about it, you really can't do anything more. You can definitely do less, but you can't push yourself farther than your best.

When you wake up and start to go over the days, weeks, and months when you were less than productive, always ask yourself, *Did I do my best in terms of the limitations depression puts on me? Am I expecting a standard that simply wasn't possible?* For example, if you only make it through a few of these strategies before you put down this book, maybe that's all you can do in the moment. *You* know what you can and can't do. Pushing yourself to do more than you're capable of is not doing your best.

This doesn't mean you just sit back and let depression decide what you can and can't do. You still have the power to make the changes you need to make, to get better and get things done. But go easy on yourself. You're doing what you can.

Here's what *not* doing your best looks like:

- You don't get out of bed and make yourself get dressed and eat breakfast.

- You use depression as an excuse for not doing the things you actually can do.

- You never start projects because you feel you won't be capable of doings things perfectly.

- You don't make an effort to do what you can in the moment.

- You're extremely self-critical about what you do get done.

Can you think of what your best looks like when you're not depressed? Is there a chance you're easier on yourself at those times? If so, use this standard to take care of yourself when your best doesn't seem like enough.

Alex's Story

When I'm well, it's so easy to get things done. How's it possible that when I'm depressed it's like walking through a really thick fog to get things done? It makes me so angry, but by simply doing what I can during the day, at least I go home knowing I did something. I can say to myself, *Alex, was it really possible for you to do more than you did? Were you truly well enough to work 12 hours today? That is just unrealistic thinking.*

I have to talk with myself and remind myself all the time that I do as much as possible. There are some days when this definitely isn't enough. I do get really hard on myself. That's just how it is. But I try to remember that I can only work as hard as my brain and body will allow.

My Story

Is there anything I could have done differently in the past about my scattered work record? I know for sure that when I was actually in a job, I always tried to work to my capacity. I was always pro- moted and never heard complaints about my actual work. It was when I got sick that things were tough. Especially because I had *no* idea what was going on.

I look back and think of all I could have done. I could have stayed at home more instead of going out drinking. I could have learned more management skills. I could have bought a lot more art! I could have learned a language! I could have done so much better! Some of this behavior was a true lack of maturity, but much of it was a way of dealing with mood swings. I drank to feel better. I did what I had to do at the time. I regret it, but don't see how, with my lack of knowledge, I could have known that much of my behavior was caused by a mental illness.

What I do now:

- I know I have an illness, so now, everything I do with full knowledge that makes me depressed is my own fault and means I'm not doing my best.

- I look at my past realistically and accept that the present is probably pretty similar to the past in terms of what my best looks like when I'm sick.

- I have friends and family who say, "Julie, you were sick. Don't be so hard on yourself. It's over. Just do things differently next time." I listen because they often have a lot more insight than I do.

- I have to, must, and will work daily on accepting that I did what I could for the past 20 years.

- As I write this, the words are flowing so much more easily than they were yesterday. I was sick yesterday but I kept working. Today, my best looks a *lot* better than yesterday, but the work still gets done.

Exercise

It might be that you've never thought of what you realistically can and can't do when you're depressed. You might not even know what your best is during these times because you're always comparing your ability to get things done with your nondepressed days. Look over the following projects and write what you can and can't do depending on your mood.

Cooking:

Nondepressed day: _____

_____

Depressed day: _____

_____

Volunteer work:

Nondepressed day: _____

_____

Depressed day: _____

_____

Cleaning the house:
Nondepressed day: _____

_____

Depressed day: _____

_____

Exercising:
Nondepressed day: _____

_____

Depressed day: _____

_____

Socializing:
Nondepressed day: _____

_____

Depressed day: _____

_____

Many times, a change in attitude helps you do your best. When you accept that your productivity might be different when you're depressed, you're able to go easier on yourself and get more things done!

ASK DR. PRESTON

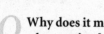

Why does it make a difference if you simply do your best when you're depressed?

The best remedy for powerlessness is taking action, and the best remedy for depressive symptoms is to succeed. Failure and giving up always throw fuel on the flames of depression. When you do your best, no matter what that means, you do succeed and there's less room for the negative thoughts that come up when you don't do anything at all. Having the goal to do your best sets you up for positive results no matter what situation you're in.

The Quality of Your Work Can Be the Same

You might be amazed to find that the work that looked and felt terrible when you were depressed actually looks and feels just fine when you're not depressed. The most important thing is to do the work anyway—and then praise yourself for doing something even though you were sick. When you do the best you possibly can, you take care of yourself. Don't fall into the trap of doing your best and then judging your performance by the standards of those who don't have depression. *You* are the standard. And when you're depressed, you can only do your best.

Here are some other thoughts to consider:

- Don't compare your work to others, especially others who aren't depressed.

- Know what your best is before you start a project. It's rarely, *I want to complete the entire project in a timely manner with excellent quality.* Everyone wants that! It just might not be true for you in certain situations. Instead, try this: *I know depression will affect my work today. I want to spend three hours on this project and do what I can to the absolute best of my ability.*

- No matter what you do, or what people say, if you know you worked at *your* ultimate depression-challenged ability, always remind yourself that you did your best.

- When you think of your past and the nasty thoughts come up of what you *could* have done, say this out loud: "I'm sad that my past wasn't what I hoped it would be. But I obviously did what I could in the moment. Things can change as of today, when I always do my best."

Remember: Always tell yourself, *Considering the circumstances, I did my best!*

34

Educate Your Friends and Family About Depression

Depression can make a lot of people silent. This might come from the shame of being so sick or from brain changes that affect expression and the desire to connect with others. When this happens to you, the people in your life can get very confused, frustrated, and worried. They might not understand what you're going through and make negative judgments about you due to limited information. The end result might be that you lose the respect of the people you care about. They want to know what's going on, but see your silence as a lack of interest in what they feel and a lack of desire to get better.

Nondepressed People Lack Information

If you broke your leg right before a 5K race, people would easily see and understand why you had to opt out of the event. You would probably share the story of how you broke the leg and how long your doctor said it will take to heal. This easily explains why you won't complete the race. But when you're depressed, you might hold back this essential information regarding why you have trouble getting things done.

Depression is not the taboo it used to be. More people are coming out and talking about their struggles with the illness as well as what medications they're taking. This new environment can help you open up about why things are so difficult for you and why you're acting as you are. When you wake up without energy, tell people why. When you start to cry in frustration because you can't concentrate, explain what you're feeling. Most importantly, when you simply can't get things done, describe the feeling in your mind and body and ask for help. The more information you give people, the easier it is for them to understand and help you when you need it most.

And that definitely beats saying, "Leave me alone! You don't understand what I'm going through." The only way your friends and family can know anything about what you're going through is if you tell them and involve them in your recovery.

Do people in your life say any of the following? If so, you might need to have a talk with them.

- "What's wrong with you? Why are you so sad? Have I done something?"
- "Why are you crying so much?"
- "I wanted to call you in here to talk about your work. Are you having trouble getting your work done?"
- "I can't take this silence anymore!"
- "Why don't you do something around the house instead of just sitting there?"
- "I love you. Please tell me what's wrong."

Listen carefully to what the people in your life are saying. They're often more aware of depression than you are.

Cole's Story

I'm very honest with my nieces and nephews about my depression. I tell them the truth when they're old enough to understand. They would be very confused otherwise, because on some days Uncle Cole can go swimming and play in the yard and help them climb trees and run around. I can *do* things with them.

When I'm depressed, I'm a bit more immobile. I tend to look at them and think, *What if something happens to them? They're so beautiful!* This is a sad time, and I used to not come around on these days. I could feel that I was missing out on a lot, but the energy it took to act well was often too much. Finally, I told them I have an illness called depression and that there will be some days when I try but just can't be as engaged as I want to be. Once, my nephew said, "Uncle Cole is sick today. We will have to play inside." He's 5. These kids understand.

Sometimes I just hug them and cry a bit. They deal with it just fine. Illness isn't so scary if you talk about it openly.

My Story

I'm extremely open about my depression with the people in my life. I can do this because I've educated them on what a bad day is like for me. They know they'll sometimes see me cry when we meet for lunch. They know I sometimes have weeks where I can't work the way I want to. There's little confusion anymore.

I used to be very negative when I was depressed. This really upset people to the point that I lost quite a few friends. I wish I had known what was going on. I just thought I was a … (you know the word!).

And I'm a very high-functioning depressed person. Because of this, the new people in my life simply won't believe that I have trouble. They say, "There is no way you're depressed! Look at what you do!" They have *no* idea.

What I do now:

- When I'm really down and I see a friend, I say, "I'm sick today." They know what that means. We still go on as though I weren't sick, but they don't expect as much from me. I work hard to focus on them when I'm down because it takes my mind off the depression.

- It took my family at least two years to learn what my depression was like and how seriously it affects my life. It was frustrating but worth it. I kept talking, and they kept listening.

- I educate people when they say something ignorant such as, "Julie, why can't you just work like a *normal* person? Everyone else does it. You're just too dramatic." Well, they need some educating, and they get it in a nice way.

Exercise

It helps if you have a stock explanation about depression you can tell people who want to know what's going on. Here are two examples:

- "When I'm depressed, everything I take pleasure in is gone. Colors are dull, and my life feels hopeless. Instead of feeling love, I feel worry and sadness. I cry very easily, no matter what's going on. I see the worst in everything. I find it almost impossible to get out of bed and just get on with my day. I need you to help me get out of the house and take a long walk."

- "When I'm depressed, everything gets on my nerves. And I mean *everything*. The way people look and walk. The seat I get in a restaurant. The door that won't open correctly. People who I wish would shut up. Traffic. I feel like beating people up, keying cars, and yelling at people who walk too slowly. This is not fun. It's really, really hard to fight because it's more of a compulsion than a choice. I promise that I work on this to the best of my ability. I need your help to point it out when it starts so we can work on it together."

Write your explanation here:

_____

_____

_____

_____

_____

ASK DR. PRESTON

Q Why does depression make it so hard to talk to others about depression?

A Most people who have had a day or two of the blues or have lost a loved one have some sense of what depression feels like. But if they haven't experienced clinical depression themselves, they can't relate to the paralysis and duration of depression. Nondepressed people have a mind-set that "time heals all wounds" and that distractions work to significantly reduce bad feelings; understanding depression just isn't in their repertoire of life experiences. They likely also have never experienced the physical symptoms of depression, such as extreme fatigue and trouble with thinking. Plus, minor bouts of the blues mainly affect emotions and thoughts and don't create the profound biological changes you see with true clinical depression.

It can be very difficult for you to explain what you go through when depression strikes. It might be easier to say nothing than to face the lack of understanding you feel you'll face if you talk to family and friends.

Of course, the other problem is that depression can either blind you to what's going on or make you feel so totally helpless that even trying to explain your experience feels impossible.

Open Up!

By teaching people about depression, you help them find compassion and understanding so they can stop judging you and move on to helping you. Your behaviors they once thought were simply lack of will power, laziness, or meanness can be seen in a new light. This takes a lot of pressure off of you and gives you more space to work on getting better and getting things done.

Say the following when the situation is appropriate:

- "When I'm depressed, I have trouble understanding what you want me to do. Please try not to be frustrated if I keep forgetting what you say. Remind me to write it down."

- "When I'm depressed, I feel no joy for my work. This is what I feel and is not necessarily true. Please remind me that I always feel this way when I'm depressed and that my love for my work will come back."

- "If you're not sure what's going on with me, ask. I can explain what my mind is saying in the moment and why I'm having such a tough time."

- "I have a lot of anxiety when I get depressed. I love it when you take me somewhere quiet and we can just talk so I can calm down."

Remember: The only person in your life who knows what's really going on is you. By teaching your friends and family what your depression looks and feels like, they'll be more able to understand and help you.

Expect to Cry

Crying is a very normal part of depression. If you didn't know this, you might ask yourself, *Why am I so weak? What is wrong with me? I never cry like this!* It's true that you might have never cried like you do when you're depressed.

Crying can be embarrassing if you're in a public place such as at work, school, or a PTA meeting. You might also cry when you think of all you have to do around the house because you feel so overwhelmed and frustrated that there's no one to help you. Depression can create a cascade of tears that can be difficult to stop.

You Can Keep Going

Both men and women cry more when they're depressed. Depending on how you were raised and what society you're from, crying can be seen as something cathartic or something embarrassing. Crying can be silent, and it can be large and noisy sobs. The amount you cry usually depends on the severity of your depression.

Even though crying feels like it will keep you from your projects, you *can* keep going until the crying stops. And it often does. You can paint, fix a car, get on a plane, and take care of children even when you're depressed and crying. (It might help to explain to the people around you why you're crying so they know it's from depression and not necessarily from a catastrophe or serious problem.) Crying is often a physical symptom of depression and often, just like an allergy, you can work through it.

Think about your crying. Do any of the following signs that crying is caused by depression apply to you?

- You cry over situations that normally don't make you cry.
- You cry even though there's nothing wrong.
- You cry much more than usual over the injustices of the world.
- It's very hard to stop crying.
- Your crying makes it hard for you to breathe.

It may help to change your views on crying and see it as a sign you need help instead of something you need to hide from others.

Patrick's Story

Unless you're a man, you probably don't realize how embarrassing it is for men to cry. I once read a book on the differences between how men and women are raised. If a little girl falls down, she's often hugged and coddled. When I fell down, I was told to *be a little man!*

This now carries over to my work. I have actually felt myself start to cry when someone says anything negative about my work. Very, very embarrassing. I've never let anyone see it, though. I once went home and had to shut my bedroom door because I was crying so hard.

I still feel that crying is stupid, weak, and ridiculous. But it's my life. I know there are some times I just don't function at work the way I want to. People might say something and I can feel the tears start. *Be a man* doesn't always work, but I still tell myself that. When I'm at work and want to hide in my office, I repeat it over and over to myself and the crying stops.

My Story

When I'm depressed, I have what I call a waterfall of tears. It's as though the floodgates in my eyes open and a lot, lot more tears pour out than usual. This used to happen when I had to work with a difficult colleague. I also remember crying in college when the professor would say something about my performance in class. Once I talked when another person was talking, and the professor sort of chastised me. I had to put on my sunglasses, I was crying so much. I wanted to run out of the room. This is one of the reasons school was difficult when I was depressed.

When I'm not depressed, I work and attend class like a normal person. In fact, I don't cry at all. Depression is so crazy and hard to understand. How is it possible that the same situation is so much harder to take when I'm depressed than when I'm well? Why do I cry so much? It's embarrassing sometimes, but I can't really stop it.

What I do now:

- I know that the "floodgate" crying is a sign I'm depressed, and it's naturally a lot harder to get things done.

- If I cry in frustration when I have a hard task, I tell myself to just keep going until it's done.

- I know that crying when I have a writing job is not a good sign and I need to really think about whether the project is right for me.

- I have what I call the sympathy sob. This happens when I see something sad and suddenly I just feel a sob rise out of my chest. I know this is a sign that I'm depressed and I need to see what's going on in my life that's causing me stress.

Exercise

Think of the last time you cried when you were depressed, and ask yourself these questions:

- What was the situation?
- Was the crying unexpected?
- Did the crying feel out of place?
- Were others scared for you?

Look over the following ideas and decide what steps you can take when you feel your crying is due to depression:

- See if a specific event led to the crying.
- Calm down and see it as a symptom of an illness, not an indication that something's necessarily wrong.
- See your doctor.
- Look at your workload and other obligations.
- Look for crying due to hormonal changes.

Crying is a sign that something's going on. It might be a normal sign of depression, or it might indicate a problem that needs to be addressed immediately.

ASK DR. PRESTON

Q **Why do depressed people cry so much?**

A Crying likely serves several purposes. Crying is a distress signal. Babies do this, and their parents are alerted to their discomfort and feed them or rock them. Likewise, crying is a social signal that might elicit support from others. Crying has been found to bring significant emotional relief.

There are basically two types of crying. One is an aborted crying spell where you try not to cry. When you hold back tears it's often accompanied by a flood of inner negative thoughts (e.g., *What's wrong with me? I'm crying like a baby* and other negative self-talk that generates shame). The other version is where you give yourself permission to cry. Rather than being self-condemning, you accept that crying is a natural and understandable human reaction to loss, disappointment, or significant stress.

Crying often leads to emotional relief for people with depression. Emotional tears contain the stress hormone ACTH (adrenocorticotropic hormone). The lowering of ACTH levels has a direct impact on the stress hormone cortisol. Cortisol levels are often significantly elevated in depression and have been found to increase depressive symptoms. If you decrease ACTH levels, cortisol levels also decrease. Thus, crying is a way to reduce the levels of this hormone and lessen depressive feelings.

Crying Is Okay

Crying is not a sign of weakness, and you can still get things done when you're crying. True, you'll probably be embarrassed, but that is okay. You just keep going. If you're a man, you might feel pressure not to cry; do it in private if you need to.

You can learn to manage, end, and prevent crying spells:

- Know exactly why you're crying. If the crying isn't attached to a concrete experience, you know you're facing depression-based crying and you can often go on with what you're doing.

- Stop a crying attack by getting on all fours and breathing while saying, "This is panic attack crying. I'm okay. This is my body's reaction, not an indication that I'm falling apart."

- Let others see you cry and explain that it's depression and will end.

- If you cry for more than a day, see a mental health professional.

Remember: Notice when you cry the most. This knowledge is a tool you can use to determine if a project is too much for you or if your depression is getting too serious for you to manage alone.

Accept the Losses Caused by Depression

It's human nature to want to make the most of your time here on Earth. Living life to the fullest is one of the greatest pleasures you can have. Unfortunately, people with depression can lose marriages, work and school opportunities, dreams, and health to this illness. The resulting sadness and feeling of mourning, especially if the loss is ongoing, can spiral a person further into depression. It's hard to live life to the fullest if something is holding you back.

Lost Time from Depression

With physical illness, it's easier to accept the fact that your injury affects the time you have to get things done. When you have the flu or are in a car accident, you often get a lot of help and sympathy as you recover. And you'll probably be pretty compassionate with yourself. But with depression, the lost time can seem so pointless. You wonder, *Where did my day go? Why didn't I try harder? What am I doing with my life?* It's easy to forget that lost time is a part of depression for everyone.

Depression takes away parts of your life that you need. It can take your productivity, your ability to connect with others, your ability to exercise like you want to, and myriad other things. On many days, you can use the strategies in this book to get through these problems, but on some days, even they won't work and you may "lose" a day. Maybe you sit around watching DVDs all day. Maybe you take a sick day from work. Maybe you miss a deadline for something you promised you would do. Some losses are much bigger. Maybe you get fired, or maybe someone you love leaves.

Losses big and small happen to everyone who has depression. The only way to get through them and move on is to accept the reality of what has happened and do all you can to minimize what depression takes away from you in the future.

What have you lost because of depression?

- Jobs?
- A university degree?
- Relationships?
- Promotions?
- Respect from others?

- Time—possibly years?
- Ability to travel?
- Enthusiasm for life?
- A positive past?
- Money?

These feelings of loss can be particularly strong if you feel you should be somewhere different because you're a certain age. If this is the case, it might be time to change your goals to ones you can accomplish.

Penny's Story

I love my son more than I can explain. I take care of him myself. I read to him, make his dinner, talk with him, and try to teach him about life. When he was born, I got really depressed. I know it was postpartum depression, and I know I was sick, but I feel so guilty. My mother came and had to take care of him for three months. I didn't want to breast-feed, and I didn't feel love for him. She made sure he was well taken care of, and luckily for me, understood that I was sick and did what she could to make sure I bonded with him. When I got on meds, I couldn't breast-feed him anymore. I was immobilized by depression. I don't think I loved him as much as I should have. I could have taken him for more walks. Sometimes I would just sit in the rocking chair with him and rock him and cry.

That was four years ago. I still get depressed off and on. I've been like this my whole life. There are days when I look at this gorgeous kid and just can't do what I'm supposed to do. I have to read to him! I have to make him a great, healthy dinner with lots of vegetables! I have to take him to the park. I have to make sure he's with other kids. On days where all this seems impossible, it's often too painful to even look at him. He's so beautiful, and I'm often so sick. Am I wrecking his life?

One day I just stopped all this. I know he knows how much I love him. He knows I have bad days, the days he gets less of my active love but all my mother love. So he eats some macaroni and cheese, and I can only read one book on some nights. He doesn't seem to mind. Sometimes this lasts for a week and I know it's a sign I need to go to my doctor; sometimes it's just one day. He seems fine. The guilt is a lot worse than the actual events. I don't want to lose a day of my time with him to depression. I lost months of his childhood, and I *won't* lose more.

My Story

Because of my depression, I'm not able to handle the stress of working with other people. I've tried it for 20 years and finally accepted that group work is not an option for me. This is such a huge loss, mostly because it keeps me from the daily human contact I really need. I still think, *Maybe I can do it now that I have these strategies. Maybe I can handle the stress a bit better.* But when I do try, I get depressed and easily stressed. It's not the work itself; it's the fact that when you work with a group, there's almost always some kind of personality clash between members of the group. I've also had the unfortunate experience of working with negative and manipulative people—more than once!

I wish I could just accept this as part of human nature, but I can't. It makes me feel desperate and sad just to think about this. Not being able to work with other people is a huge loss for me. Writing is a lonely career for people like me, but it's less stressful than a management position, for example. So I try to focus on what I *can* do. It's hard, but I'm in my 40s now, and it's not realistic to ignore more than 20 years of very plain facts. I work the best I can, and that's what I have to focus on.

What I do now:

- I recognize that the more than 20 years I spent searching for reasons why I wasn't as productive as I could have been are over and I will never get them back.

- I accept that I have a lot of lost time to look forward to in my future, but because I'm managing my depression much better, I can shorten this time.

- I lost a marriage because of my mood swings and more jobs and friends than I can count. This is sad, but I've finally accepted this, which is how I could move on. (It took many years, but it's better than staying in the same sad place forever.)

Exercise

On a piece of paper, make a list of all the ways depression has taken your time and life energy in the past. Write down all the relationships and work opportunities it has ruined. Write down all the ways it's impacted your life.

Now wad up the paper and throw it in the garbage. Those days are never coming back. The best way to manage depression so you can be productive is to keep trying so you'll have much fewer big losses in the future.

ASK DR. PRESTON

Q **Why is it so hard—and sad—to accept the fact that depression is an illness that can take so much away from you?**

A Losses—the loss of a dream, the loss of a childhood, or the loss of productive years—are common with depression, and it's natural to mourn those losses. But it's important to face the truth of painful losses—not wallowing in it or becoming obsessively preoccupied, but squarely facing the loss. Facing the grief you feel at such losses is probably best done with the companionship of another person such as a trusted friend or therapist.

The tears and anguish that accompany loss and mourning are signs of how important the loss is; they are a way the mind and body acknowledge the truth that "this mattered deeply to me." Robert Frost said, "The best way out is through," and when you can come to terms with the losses depression can cause, you've probably done some amount of working through your grief, but hopefully not by getting bogged down with anger and bitterness. It's much more productive—and honest—to reframe the big losses from, "He shouldn't just walk out on a 25-year marriage!!!" to something more like, "He did walk out and it hurts so much!"

When enough grieving can take place, things start to seem more settled and that's when you can turn your attention to the present and a future of new opportunities.

You're Not Giving Up

When you focus only on what you've lost, it's difficult to change things so your future looks and is more positive. You don't have to be super optimistic and happy all the time, but you do have to be forward-thinking in order to counteract the way depression may have robbed you in the past. As with any serious illness, you can experience great loss. But you can also experience great future productivity when you accept the losses of the past.

Here are some other thoughts to consider:

- When you feel yourself dwelling on the past and all that you've lost, feel it as intensely as you can and get it out of your system.

- Be ready to face more losses in the future—maybe a lot more losses. They're a reality of depression and life in general. On the days when you get into bed at night and realize you've lost another day and feel helpless and hopeless, remind yourself, *These lost days happen, but I don't have to lose another one tomorrow.*

- Know that the past is *never* coming back. There's a good chance that your loss is forever, and it's time to build a new life.

- Having said the above, you can fix some losses once you manage depression and are more able to work effectively.

Remember: Depression creates loss, but acceptance creates hope. Focus on what you can fix, and let the other stuff go forever.

Set Outside Limits

Trying to meet all your obligations when you're depressed is often impossible. There are so many ways you can feel overwhelmed, especially when it comes to getting things done on time. You might quit and then feel disgusted with yourself not only for quitting, but for not being able to control the situation in the first place.

The depressed brain is a confused brain. Asking yourself to set time limits on your work is a very good idea, but it's not always possible. It might be that you can't even focus on the work itself, much less get something done in the time it needs to be completed.

Look Outside for Help

There's a good chance you have people and organizations in your life that can help you limit or increase the time you spend on a project. Maybe your work gives you deadlines or your children have to be certain places at certain times. Although this might feel like too much pressure, in reality, these outside limits can greatly help your productivity by taking away the worry that you won't get something done the way it needs to get done.

Is there someone or something in your life that can work as your taskmaster? Maybe it's an organization or a person. It may be limited hours at a place you want to work, such as a room in a library that's available for only two hours. It may be working with a friend who will hold you to your schedule. It may be asking someone at work to keep you focused so you can finish a project on time. However you find the limits, the more you can set up, the more you can get done when you're depressed.

The following are signs you need outside limits; do you recognize any in yourself?

- Setting deadlines for yourself doesn't work.
- You feel guilty that you're always late with projects.
- You work better with a team.
- You respond well to others telling you what to do.

Depression can make you feel that others will say no if you ask for help in setting limits in your life. In reality, many people will gladly help. You just have to ask.

Ariel's Story

I know that when I'm depressed, I won't get to work on time if I rely only on an alarm. I have enough trouble staying out of bed in the afternoon; getting out of bed in the morning to go to work is often impossible. I used to be late a lot. That's not exactly a good practice when I have enough trouble just getting through the workday when I'm depressed.

I've solved this problem in three ways. I started to carpool with people who expect a lot from me. I ask both of them to call me when they get up. I bought a really loud, old-fashioned alarm—the kind with the bells on the top that are hit by a little hammer. And I talked with my boss and told him I need to be held accountable when I have a deadline. He's fine with that. I don't want to let down any of these people. This is not pressure for me but support.

My Story

Thank heavens for publishing deadlines. I know my work would drag on forever if I didn't have a whole group of people expecting my manuscript at a certain time. It's the only way I can write books and get them on the market. My deadlines can be intense, but still, they help organize my brain because I know that no matter what, whether I'm depressed or well, people are depending on me. If I feel too depressed to work, I know that if I don't have a deadline, I'll end up talking with a friend, going to lunch, feeling sorry for myself, and doing everything except my work. That, in turn, makes me a lot more depressed. I feel better if I know I have to turn in a project at a very specific time.

What I do now:

- I focus on the date I'm given and force myself to take the deadline very seriously. I remind myself that getting out of it is not an option.

- If I truly am too sick to work, I look at my days carefully and know how long I can put something off. If that's not possible, I talk to my editor and ask for an extension. Then I stick to that deadline.

182

- I get help from a variety of people and organizations by letting them know my problem and how they can help. I say, "Get on my case! Call me and let me know when you expect something to get back to you."

- I know that I do my most creative and calm work if someone or something else limits my work time.

Exercise

Find your personal taskmaster. Working with someone who is very precise about time is a good way to get yourself on track when you're depressed. Think about the people in your life. Who likes calendars, deadlines, watches, and handheld devices that tell them where they are every minute of the day? That person might be a very good taskmaster for you!

List the tasks you need to get done and show this person the list:

1. _____

2. _____

3. _____

Get out a calendar and go over it with your taskmaster. Ask him or her to call you and check in on certain dates. Set a time once a week to meet and go over your progress. This works especially well when you work with a therapist or group.

ASK DR. PRESTON

Why does depression often respond to outside limitations and obligations?

Limits are tremendously important and effective. You can have all kinds of good intentions when you want to do something, yet moments before going out to eat, working out, or going shopping, the immediate sensation often is one of fatigue, despair, and a lack of motivation. Even something as simple as getting off the couch is very hard to do in such moments. Once you get moving, though, it feels easier. The obligation to meet a friend, for example, puts extra pressure on the task and makes it a powerful incentive for you to get moving.

Get Others to Help Your Work

Being open to outside limits helps you get work done. Period. Your goal is to put yourself in a situation where someone or something forces you to work even when you feel depressed. Having an outside deadline helps you focus on what you *can* do instead of what you *can't* do. When you feel unable to clean your house, have someone come over who kicks your behind and makes you focus on your work so you can have coffee together when your house is clean. Ask people at work to kindly remind you that a deadline is coming up. Put yourself in a place where an organization is depending on you. Do what you can to leave the timeline to others so you can finally have some relief from the pressure of having to do things by yourself all the time.

Here are some other thoughts to consider:

- If you're on a committee or have to work in a group, let others set your work timelines and tell them you want extra help to get them done. You can then focus on the work itself.

- Ask a friend to drop you off at work and pick you up at a specific time.

- Join a club where people write, work out, sing, fix things, learn a craft, golf, sail, and generally do things in groups so they can decide when you come and go.

- Set outside limits that are reasonable for you so you don't quit and go back to your old ways.

Remember: When depression doesn't allow you to be your own taskmaster, find someone or something that can.

Get Some Exercise

Action and human contact can help reduce the symptoms of depression. Exercise is the best way to do both. But getting out and taking action is one of the main difficulties you face when you're depressed. As with many of your depression symptoms, you have to work to make positive changes when you're in the middle of a downswing, but exercise is so imperative to depression management that any effort you can make is well worth it.

Just Twenty Minutes a Day

Numerous research studies substantiate the idea that exercise helps depression. Most importantly, the research also indicates that it doesn't take much exercise to make a difference. Just 20 minutes a day can help you get out and get something done. Depressed people often feel greater stress and get down on themselves for longer than the time it takes to actually get out and exercise. Remind yourself of this.

A good, brisk walk, for example, is one of the best treatments for depression. You might never want to walk when you're depressed, but you'll almost always feel better after you walk. You don't have to walk far, and you don't have to enjoy the walk (though you probably will after you start), but it's important that you get outside and move your legs and swing your arms at least once a day. The more endorphins you can create, the better you'll feel.

Do any of these signs you need to exercise ring true to you?

- You're overweight, and that alone makes you more depressed, which makes you sit around instead of getting things done.
- You've stopped participating in a sport you used to love.
- Sitting in front of the television just isn't working for you.
- You're alone way too much and want to be with people.
- You want to improve your mood *while* getting something done.

Robert's Story

When my wife left me, my life fell apart. My work suffered, and I was depressed for the first time in my life. I now understand what a few of my friends have gone through. Before the breakup, I'd had down times, but never a depression like this. It was terrible. It went on for months and months and seemed like it would never end. I would go into the restaurant where I work and knew I *had* to work. I had customers who depended on me. This helped set up parameters that kept me getting out of bed.

That wasn't enough, though, so I started working out—every single day after work, even when I didn't want to. Every day. I lifted weights and took a spinning class. Then I started to run. I noticed results in my mood after a month, and saw a definite change in my body after a few months. I always felt better after I worked out. My energy increased at work. I actually started to look forward to things, and my depression started to lessen. It took a full year for me to consider myself fully recovered. I have no idea where I would be now without the exercise. And the best thing? At 50, I have the best body of my life. I now work out with weights three to four times a week and run as much as I can.

My Story

I know exercise makes me feel better. It's getting started that's the problem. On the depressed days, I have trouble changing into my walking shoes—that's how nonfunctioning I feel. I had shoulder surgery last year, and that really threw me off. I saw the difference that lack of exercise made within a few months—not only weight gain, but a lack of physical well-being. I need to exercise if I want to feel better. I want to focus on the good stuff: improved body and mood!

What I do now:

- I tell myself, *Just put on your shoes and walk, Julie. Stop thinking about it and do it. You say you want to be less depressed and work on your book. This is one way to do it.*

- I signed up to take swimming lessons with my nephew. Being in the pool on a sunny day with children is amazingly good for the mood. And I have to accept that *no one* cares what I look like in a bathing suit.

- I walk with a friend.

- I cut out pictures from magazines of people exercising as well as those who have lost a lot of weight and put them on my refrigerator for inspiration.

- I see a physical therapist to deal with my shoulder injury. My goal is to do yoga again.

Exercise

Healthy exercise always makes you feel better. When you're depressed, getting started is often the biggest obstacle. One solution is to pick an exercise that feels right for you.

Look over the following list and check the exercise (or exercises) that looks appealing:

☐ Aerobics	☐ Running
☐ Baseball/softball	☐ Sitting in front of the TV (Hey! This is a joke!)
☐ Biking	☐ Soccer
☐ Fencing	☐ Swimming
☐ Football/flag football	☐ Tai chi/chi gong
☐ Golf	☐ Triathlon
☐ Hiking	☐ Ultimate Frisbee
☐ Horseback riding	☐ Volleyball
☐ Marathon running	☐ Walking with a friend or in a group
☐ Martial arts	☐ Weight training
☐ Rock/mountain climbing	☐ Yoga

Now, what exercise will you start first? You might not want to do any of them, but you know you can't wait until you *want* to feel like doing something. You just have to take the first step and do it!

ASK DR. PRESTON

Q Why does action help depression?

A At the heart of depression is a perception of powerlessness and helplessness. Action is the antidote for powerlessness. Seeing that you're moving, working, and getting things done in the moment can combat the ever-present sense of powerlessness depression brings.

Exercise causes an elevation in mood that makes it much easier to keep going once you get started. Many other tasks and routines don't have this immediate mood-boosting effect. Cleaning the house or paying bills might feel good after you get them done, but in the midst of the task, you don't have the increased mood like you do with exercise.

Exercise can also help you have essential human contact that may be lacking when you're depressed.

Do What's Best for You

It's very important that you set up an exercise program you know will work for you. For some people, going to the gym is a helpful, doable regimen. For others, just the thought of getting all the clothes ready, driving to the gym, getting changed, and then having to take a shower afterward is just too much. Pick an exercise that will *work for you*.

Here are some other thoughts to consider:

- What exercise do you like? This has nothing to do with what's currently popular in gyms across the country. Some bodies were made to walk; some were made for tae kwon do. What have you always thought would be fun to try? It's pretty much a given that you won't continue with what you don't like.

- Choose an exercise that *always* makes you feel better when you're done, and focus on that feeling instead of how hard it is to get started.

- Exercise in a group if you tend to isolate yourself.

- Choose something you feel comfortable doing, not something that makes you feel inadequate or ashamed of your body.

- Set up an exercise schedule when you're well that you have to stick to when you're depressed.

- Hire a coach, explain your situation, and pay ahead. You'll have support and be more likely to go because you already spent the money.

Remember: You might never feel like exercising when you're sick, but after you do the exercise, you won't say, "Gee! I wish I hadn't done that!" If anything, you'll be proud of yourself that you did it.

Pay to Get the Help You Need

The natural pessimism and lethargy that come with depression can work against you in many ways, especially in how you use your money to make life easier when you're depressed. You might feel reluctant to pay someone else to get things done when you're depressed. You might not feel worthy of getting the much-needed help money can buy, and the act of actually setting up appointments and taking the time to buy what you need might feel overwhelming. You might also feel outside pressure to do the work yourself, as it's "not a big deal to do these things!" as some people ignorant of depression might point out.

Let Your Money Work for You

If you're lucky enough to be someone who doesn't have to worry about money when you're depressed, using this money to help you get things done is a necessity. It's easy to be really hard on yourself when you're depressed, "should"ing yourself all over the place: *I can't pay $100 for someone to clean my house! I should be able to do it myself! I don't want to pay for someone to do my yard. I should be able to cut my roses and prune my trees myself! I don't need to hire a tutor! I should easily pass a physics class by myself!* The *should*s are a dangerous part of depression. You have to ignore them and use your money.

One way to be sure the help is there when you need it is to put it in motion when you're well. Call and set up an appointment, think of money, put up an ad, and interview someone when you're well, when your brain is better able to process the steps. These tasks don't come easily when you're depressed, but they are easy when you're well. If setting up help when you're well isn't possible, you have to push yourself to get help in the moment when you need it. Focus on the relief you'll feel when something gets done, even if you pay someone else to do it for you.

Look over the following signs to see if you might need to spend money to get some help:

- The thought of preparing dinner every night is overwhelming.

- Your work requires research that could be done by another person.

- The little tasks that need to get done overwhelm the projects.

- You feel too guilty to spend money, so you get nothing accomplished.

Instead of focusing on the process of paying and the money used, think of the end result and the energy saved.

Laila's Story

I run my own public-relations business. I usually have a lot of fun with my work, and I definitely make plenty of money. Last year, my son got sick and almost died, and I went into a deep depression. Even when he got better, I couldn't shake it. It's as though his illness forced me to really look at my life, such as the fact that I often worked more than 50 hours a week. People were always telling me that I should stop trying to be super-mom. My husband helped a lot, but I still felt I had to clean the house, make all the dinners, and bake cookies for my son's band fund-raisers. No one told me to do this! I thought it made me a better mom.

Something happened when I realized he was going to be okay. I hired someone to do the yard. I started to buy prepared food. I bought cookies or just made a donation. I hired a weekly housekeeper who also takes care of my plants. And I made one really, really big decision: I hired a junior PR agent. Now I have more time for my son. I actually work less, and my depression was gone within six months.

My Story

Five years ago, I started a web page selling downloadable books. It really took off—more than I thought it would. At first I worked much more than I had ever been able to work, just to keep up with the orders and the e-mails. I thought I had to answer every single e-mail I received asking questions about mental health. I used to give a detailed answer to each one—and there were often more than 20 a day. When I thought about not answering some, I'd think, *But what will the person think of me if I don't answer!* and continued typing away.

Keeping busy was great for me in many ways, and not being in an office setting made it possible for me to work a lot more than usual. But then the depression caught up with me. I also had a lot of anxiety. I would wake up and think of all the work I had to do and how the e-mail was like an avalanche. Eventually I got behind as I got more worried and depressed. When I got my first book deal, I was excited, but I realized there was no way I could do both. My family and friends kept telling me to hire someone, but I was sure there was no way a person could learn the business, as the work I was doing online was so new. And how would I possibly pay this person? I didn't have a lot of cash lying around.

But I took the advice and hired a business manager. Hiring Laura was the smartest decision of my work life. Three years later she still runs what I now call "our" web page. She makes her salary every month by her creative work on the site. I don't wake up worrying about the business anymore. Now I just worry about the books!

What I do now:

- I pay my manager what she deserves and try to give regular bonuses. I would not have my business without her.

- I eat out a lot when I'm not feeling my best. I do think it's a waste of money in the long run, but I need the break from cooking.

- I have someone mow my lawn.

- I am working really hard on the "I should be able to do this" stuff. I know my limitations and have to talk back to that language. If I have to pay for something, such as using a drive-through car wash, I do it.

Exercise

List five areas in your life where you simply don't want to or can't do what has to be done such as cooking, yard work, house cleaning, etc. The tasks that make you feel overwhelmed are usually the ones where you need the most outside help.

1. _____

2. _____

3. _____

4. _____

5. _____

Next, let go of your reluctance and the depression talk that keeps you trapped in having to do things you can't really do. Do any of these sound familiar?

- *I really should be able to do the small things! They're so simple.*
- *I have plenty of time to do what I need to do. Getting help is self-indulgent.*
- *My partner doesn't understand.*
- *What if it takes all of my money?*
- *I've never really spent money on myself.*
- *It probably won't help my depression anyway.*
- *It just feels too hard to even get things started. Hiring someone feels impossible.*

Choose one area in your life where you can hire someone to do the work for you. Write the work here and the first step you need to take.

Work: _____

First step: _____

ASK DR. PRESTON

Q **Why does depression make you loath to spend money on things that would make life so much easier, such as hiring a cleaner or buying ready-made food?**

A When you're depressed, you experience profound pessimism. You may say you know hiring someone to clean your house would help, but inwardly you might think, *What's the use? It won't make any difference in how I feel.* And even if you decided to hire some help, the prospect of having to call several people or do the legwork to locate an appropriate person can feel too daunting. Low energy and lack of motivation keep you frozen in your tracks. Or maybe you don't feel like you're worth it. Maybe on some level you feel you're not worthy enough to splurge on hiring a housekeeper.

Spend the Money!

There are many ways you can use money to make your life much easier when you're depressed:

Go to restaurants or buy ready-made food. You have plenty of very nutritious ready-made food options. Some stores even sell deliciously prepared vegetables and meats. Restaurants are quick and healthy choices, as are comfort food–style restaurants you can hit when you're depressed. And getting something delivered is *not* a sign your kids are not fed correctly, and you're not lazy if you take prepared food to work seven days a week.

Go to therapy. Therapy might seem expensive, but if you have the funds, what you learn in terms of getting things done even when you're depressed can far outweigh the cost of the therapist. When you have the funds, not seeing a therapist (or any person who can make you feel better when you're down, such as a masseuse) because you think it's too expensive may not be a realistic choice. Measure the cost of being depressed and what financial strains that may put on you versus seeing a therapist in order to get things done and bring in more money.

Hire a babysitter. There are many things you can do to improve productivity if you work at home, and hiring a babysitter is one of the best, even if the sitter is there while you work. If you have a project due or a term paper to write, for example, think of the financial cost if the work doesn't get done and weigh that against the cost of a sitter. It might seem odd to pay someone so you can be home alone, and doing this may make you feel more depressed if you feel you "don't even have enough energy to take care of my kids like I normally do," but getting the work done is the goal.

Hire an exercise professional. You have many options when it comes to exercise: you can hire a personal trainer, a yoga teacher to come to your house, a Pilates instructor, a golf pro, a dietician, or you can go to a spa! This all can help depression. It might take an individual professional to get you started on a program. When you pay a professional trainer, you're more likely to use them, especially if they come to your house.

Remember: Having enough money to use on conveniences is a real gift when you're depressed. Hiring someone to make things easier on you is not a weakness or a waste of money. If the extra help helps you, it's worth it. Depression makes you think you should do it all and then takes away your ability to do things with ease. When you pay someone to do what you can't, you've beaten depression once again!

Tackle One Project at a Time

For some depressed people, it might be easier to start a project than actually see it to completion. When you're depressed, the initial rush of getting something started can be a bit of a high. You might feel enthusiasm and a belief that maybe *for once* things will be okay. In other instances, you're forced through work or other obligations to perform a task in addition to your current work, such as when you sign up for a volunteer position. However, when the reality of the work hits you, you run out of steam and things come to a halt.

Fight the Desire to Do Everything at Once

When you're depressed and under a deadline, you often think you have to do everything at once. This can be very stressful and unproductive if you're having attention-deficit hyperactivity disorder (ADHD) symptoms as well. You might flit from one project to another without really accomplishing anything. This can be so frustrating and can often cause you to stop because you feel so confused and overwhelmed. It might be that doing one project at a time is not exactly the way depression makes you behave. Instead, it makes you think you must get everything done at once and that you're a failure if you don't.

Luckily, there's a way around this. You have to forget *all* that you have to do, pick *one* project (the smaller the project the better at first), and do it until you're done. You don't get to start anything else until the first project is completely done. This creates the focus you need to see something through even when your brain isn't functioning properly.

Do any of these signs you need to do one project at a time ring true for you?

- You have huge to-do lists.
- You have many artistic projects all around the house that you just can't seem to complete.
- You're having work troubles because you jump from project to project.

- You feel bored or overwhelmed with a project so you move on to the next to feel better. As a result, you rarely get the satisfied feeling that comes with completing a project.

- You're used to getting things done all at once and are really hard on yourself when this doesn't happen.

Think of one step as a whole project. This can help your feeling of accomplishment when the step actually gets done!

Sharon's Story

I write technical manuals for a large computer company. I definitely have trouble multitasking when I'm not in top form. On most days, my co-workers throw project after project on my desk—of course, it's all "urgent"! I used to try to do it all at once, often staying until late at night. I had trouble deciding what really needed to get done and was very distracted when I did start because I was sure I picked the wrong project.

I now have a new plan. I keep a sign-up list on my desk. When someone has a project, he or she adds their name and the project's needs on the list. They can see who is in front of them. I make it clear that I finish the first project on the list and then move on. I remind them that this makes me far, far more productive. I work fewer hours, and I know the great feeling of handing over something complete in a timely way.

My Story

I can still remember the lists I used to make before I realized that my problem was depression. I never had enough hours to do what I wanted to do in a day. Because of this, I got *nothing* finished. I had a trail of unfinished book ideas, incomplete sewing projects, filed attempts to organize my kitchen, unplanted flower bulbs, blah, blah, blah.

When I look back, I think there was never even a reason to make the lists except to make myself think I could be productive. Then my therapist said, "Julie, you get to have one big to-do thing on your list done each day. And it has to get done before you're allowed to move on." I've never forgotten what she said. I still struggle with this constantly, considering that depression is not an illness that encourages completion of anything, but I will never stop trying.

What I do now:

- I can tell what days are going to be good days, and I make sure I do the hard stuff then—especially the things that require an organized mind.

- I write out the steps and do them in order. This means I still get to make my much-loved lists, but I now know they will get done.

- I know I'm not allowed to start another book project until the current one is done. It's amazing how much more appealing another project is when I'm in the middle of something that's due to a publisher.

Exercise

Look over your filing system, grocery list, exercise plan, or whatever else you feel you have to do in a week. Look for areas where you're dallying with a few steps without getting something completely done. Choose one of these projects. Write out in order all you need to do with this one project.

Project: _____

1. _____
2. _____
3. _____
4. _____
5. _____

Set a time to get it done, and do the first step. Don't stop until you have all the steps done. Keep the steps small, and keep going by forcefully telling yourself that you are a person who completes projects, not someone who never gets anything done!

ASK DR. PRESTON

Q **Why does depression make you jump from project to project so you rarely get anything done effectively?**

A Higher mental functions that are dependent on the frontal lobes are required for planning, monitoring ongoing behavior, and staying organized. Very low levels of metabolic activity in these parts of the brain may account for why you jump around to projects instead of getting one done. There's also the physically uncomfortable feeling that comes with being agitated, which makes it difficult for you to stay in one place. Finally, the lack of enthusiasm so characteristic of depression makes the current work seem pointless, so you often move on to feel better. Unfortunately, it doesn't work.

One Is Not the Loneliest Number!

Some of the work you have to do definitely requires that you work on many projects at the same time. However, it's rarely the case that you have to do a little bit on each one, in order, to get finished. Most projects lend themselves to completing *one* thing fully and then moving on.

Here are some other thoughts to consider:

- Choose the small projects first, finish them, and see what you feel like after. That feeling of accomplishment is part of your reward. Keep it in mind as you work through the tougher tasks in front of you.

- Use the strategies in this book: work with a friend (Strategy 23), work when you don't feel like working (Strategy 1), set time limits (Strategy 17), just sit down and do it (Strategy 19), and always remember to be your own drill sergeant (Strategy 6)!

- If you can, only have the material you need for one project with you. Don't bring or get out any other work.

- Finishing one project when you're depressed can give you hope and energy for the next.

Remember: Focus on one project until it's done. Then, when you see you *can* finish something, you're more likely to get the next project done with ease.

Get Help for Anxiety

Research shows that well over 50 percent of people with depression experience anxiety. Anxiety *really* gets in the way of productivity, especially if you get anxious from deadlines or working with other people. On top of your depression, which is bad enough, the anxiety can feel unbelievably overwhelming. When you add worry, a racing heart, and a true fear that something is going to go wrong, getting things done may feel impossible.

Anxiety Is a Work Stopper

Anxiety often comes in waves, and sometimes you can feel it well up as soon as you have a new task to complete. Anxiety can make your body uncomfortable, affect your breathing, and make your heart beat so fast you're sure there's something physically wrong with you. It's definitely hard to keep going on a project when you feel physically ill, but it's important to recognize anxiety for what it is—a physical reaction to a specific problem *you can control.*

The more adept you become at using the strategies in this book to get things done, the greater your chances your anxiety will be reduced significantly. Seeing what you *can* do versus what you anxiously fear you'll never be able to do helps you relax and get more things done with ease.

Are any of these signs you have trouble with anxiety familiar?

- Breathing problems
- Feeling crowded
- Feeling uncomfortable in your body
- Feelings of claustrophobia (fear of closed spaces) and agoraphobia (fear of open spaces)

What does your anxiety feel like? It may be that you were not even aware you had the problem. Now that you know, changes can be made to help the symptoms.

Albert's Story

I've had panic attack feelings at big sports events, at crowded movies, at parties, when driving to a place I don't know, and under work deadlines. It's especially bad if I have an obligation I know I have to meet or else. I have trouble breathing, and once thought I was having a heart attack.

I never associated this with depression. I see my depression as a lethargic feeling, like I have trouble getting out of bed. When I thought about it, I realized that I often feel like something is wrong when I'm down. I feel a buzzing feeling and a lot of worry that it's affecting my work. Work just isn't very rewarding when I feel lousy and then feel anxious on top of that.

My first sign that I'm anxious is my breathing. I've started doing yoga on my lunch break. Just to get all that air in and out really helps. It helps with the depression, too. I'm more productive in the afternoon when I breathe a lot more.

My Story

I have a *lot* of anxiety. In fact, all the symptoms listed in the following "Exercise" section are my own. I feel anxiety in response to stressful projects, such as when I have a book due. But I also get it in really dumb situations such as when a friend calls and asks me to go to lunch when I have a deadline. I've gotten anxious because I have to find a parking place. I constantly worry that I'll be late and I'll miss something. I clench my jaw and tend to get very, very impatient with the people in my life. If they ask me something when I'm depressed, I snap at them. They don't deserve this at all. I was like this for years and didn't know why.

The anxiety is often in response to something outside myself, but I never know what's going to trigger it. On some days, I can write without worry; on others, I'm so anxious I can hardly sit and I feel that nothing's going right. It's very uncomfortable. My last book caused me a lot of terrible anxiety, and I ended up stopping the project to protect my health. I want to get things done, but not when they're so stressful I can't do them!

What I do now:

- I talk to myself: *Julie, this is a normal project. You're anxious because you have depression. Is there any doubt you can get this done? I didn't think so. Just sit for a minute and breathe.*

*Remind yourself that you've done all of this before and you can
do it again.*

- I try not to let the anxiety go into a panic attack. I do this
  by taking an antianxiety medication if I feel an attack
  coming on.

- I breathe instead of hyperventilating.

- If I have a panic attack in front of other people, I try to
  reassure them of what it is. If I'm bent over crying and
  hyperventilating, I say, "It's okay. I'm having a panic attack.
  It's okay." This helps all of us. The attacks scare my mother if
  I have one when I'm with her, but she's getting used to them.

Exercise

Knowing what happens in your body when you feel anxiety can make
it a lot easier to either accept or get more help for what you're feeling.
Look over the following list and check the anxiety symptoms you
experience when you're depressed:

- ☐ Can't breathe or have trouble catching your breath
- ☐ Simple tasks feel like too much
- ☐ Sighing or constantly blowing out your breath
- ☐ Guilt and worry
- ☐ Feeling like you will pass out
- ☐ Overall anxious feeling that something is wrong or that some-
  thing bad is going to happen
- ☐ Sleeping trouble due to worried thoughts
- ☐ Can't relax
- ☐ Everything is seen as much larger and worse than it actually is
- ☐ Feeling teary
- ☐ Full-blown panic attack: sobbing, feels impossible to breathe,
  feels like you're having a heart attack

Now ask yourself what tasks make your anxiety worse. What happens
at work that brings on anxiety? What happens with obligations?
Having to plan for or going to an event? Are you on an antidepressant

that could cause anxiety? The better you know the first signs of anxiety, the better you can help yourself catch it before it goes too far.

If you continue to feel these symptoms when you're not depressed, talk with a health-care professional about getting help for general anxiety.

Ask Dr. Preston

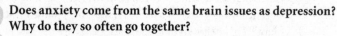

Q **Does anxiety come from the same brain issues as depression? Why do they so often go together?**

A Anxiety involves very different brain structures than depression. About 25 percent of people with major depression have a diagnosable anxiety disorder, while another 25 percent have significant anxiety that's considered a part of depression itself. Thus, depression can definitely have symptoms of anxiety without there being a separate disorder. With chronic low-grade depression, also known as *dysthymia,* about 50 percent of people have co-existing generalized anxiety disorder.

It's also common for people living with panic disorder, crippling social anxiety, post-traumatic stress disorder, and obsessive-compulsive disorder to develop a secondary or "reactive" depression in response to the havoc the anxiety causes in their lives. In other words, ruined relationships, work problems, or intense social anxiety can make people feel perpetually isolated and lonely. This can lead to and definitely increase depression.

Anxiety Is Treatable

There's some good news about anxiety. Because it's often considered a part of depression, when you're less depressed, you might find that the anxiety is a lot less as well. Anxiety can also be effectively managed through behavioral changes and exercise. A naturopath, masseuse, or yoga class can make a difference as well.

Here are some other thoughts to consider:

- Anxiety is often linked to outside events—getting lost on a backroad, being asked to talk in front of people, having too much to do, worrying about your kids, etc. Your job is to differentiate between the anxiety that's a normal reaction to life's problems versus the anxiety that often feels out of control and is only present when you're depressed.

- Work on acceptance and tolerance when you're anxious by being aware of what's going on and telling others, "I'm anxious right now. I need a break and will be right back."

- If you need to go home, go home. But think of the consequences. Being alone might be worse. Taking a break is often all you need.

- Anxiety is a bodily reaction and does not always mean something's wrong. Look around and see if your worries are real. If they're not, keep going and work through the anxiety.

Remember: Anxiety is a normal part of depression for many people, but if the anxiety doesn't get better, talk with a doctor and see what's medically available to help.

Watch What You Say

I can't. You don't understand. It's too hard. You have no idea what it's like for me! People are always trying to cheat me. I get so sick and tired of the way people drive! My manager is a jerk. I'm too tired. I don't like it here—I'm leaving. Depression makes me like this. I don't have the energy. This food is no good. This seat isn't comfortable. Why does this always happen to me? They aren't showing me the respect I deserve. I don't know how. I don't drink too much! Stop telling me what to do all the time. I'll get out of the house when I want to! I'm not negative, I'm just realistic. I can't get things done! JUST LEAVE ME ALONE!

You Are What You Say

Depression makes you say things the people around you might not understand or might not want to hear. Often you say such things because you go on autopilot when you're depressed. You're like a doll, and when your string is pulled, a prerecorded message plays over and over again, spewing gossip, anger, sadness, hopelessness, irritation, and self-pity. You might not notice this when you're depressed, but it happens. When depression is pulling your string, there's a good chance the people who care about you just can't take it anymore and leave. This is especially difficult if what you say affects your work environment.

From this day forward, look at what you say when you're depressed and decide to either keep it inside, write it down in a journal, or change it before it comes out of your mouth. Your mood may stay the same; you may still agree with what you want to say, but don't say it. This will change your life. When you have more control over what you say, you'll find that a miracle happens: the thoughts that control your words have nowhere to go, and they start to dry up. Like weeds, they need to be watered. Not saying them out loud kills them and gives you either space to say kind and positive words instead, or the simple and liberating choice to just be silent if you don't have anything positive to say.

Do any of these signs you might need to watch what you say apply to you?

- People avoid you.
- The people around you try to change the conversation to something more positive.
- People ask you why you're so negative.
- *You* don't like how you sound and know it's not the real you.
- You gossip.
- You always need to be right.
- You just don't say anything nice.

You can learn to modify what comes out of your mouth. If you start practicing today, you can take care of the problem in just a few months. The people in your life will thank you!

Peter's Story

In the past, if you tried to talk with me about politics or anything that involved opinions, I would get really loud and aggressive. This might seem simply like a personality trait, but it's not. It happens mostly when I feel agitated and down. When my life is too stressful, I snap at people. I've been written up at work about it. But that's not the real me. Friends would tell me about something they were working on and I'd tell them why it wouldn't work. I thought I was just being helpful. When they made suggestions on how I could feel better, their ideas sounded crazy and I would say, "I can't do that! That won't work!"

I think it was hardest on my family. They never knew how I would talk about certain topics because I was so up and down. It took a rather serious problem at work to get me to examine my behavior. My boss came in and said there had been complaints about my attitude. My first thought was, *I'll show you attitude!* and then suddenly I had the feeling that this wasn't the real me. I didn't want to be this person. I see that my depression is exacerbated by my anger. I'm working on both.

My Story

I have a distinct memory of walking up a flight of stairs to a sports bar with my friend Gwynn more than 10 years ago. I was complaining about something, as I always did, and she turned to me and said, "God! Can you ever say anything positive?" I knew I had a negativity problem, but was I that bad? I also remember a time on a train in Japan when I was with a group of my girlfriends. I was going on and on about how crowded the train was and how hot it was and how my clothes were uncomfortable. A friend from India turned to me and said, "Then either move home or lose some weight. Just stop talking about it all of the time!" Wow!

I wish I could say I changed at that moment, but I didn't. It would be a few years before I realized depression had distorted my feelings and led me to say the negative, whiny, and ugly things I used to say. I gossiped, envied others, complained about everything, and was generally an unpleasant person to be around.

What I do now:

- I always have days when I could just yell and yell and scream at how I hate my life and will never find happiness. But I also know that can't possibly be true. My life is not so awful when I'm well. I write these thoughts in my journal or I work all day on depression management. Complaining about my life all day is pointless.

- I no longer say things out loud unless I've thought about them a lot first. This took years of practice.

- I'm currently working as hard as possible on finding the positive in my life and saying those thoughts out loud.

Exercise

Let it all out once and for all. Write down the top 10 nasty, whiny, unhappy, weepy, angry, negative, and generally unpleasant things you say when you're depressed:

1. _____
2. _____
3. _____
4. _____
5. _____
6. _____
7. _____

8. _____

9. _____

10. _____

You are no longer allowed to say these things out loud. You can instead do the following:

- Keep quiet and focus on the other person.

- If you do say one of these, turn to the person you're with and say, "I'm sorry. I'm working on being more positive."

- Say the opposite of the nasty thought.

ASK DR. PRESTON

Q **Why do people say such awful, negative, and thoughtless things when they're depressed?**

A Depression can lead people to say mean things to themselves and to others. Most people experiencing depression are living with a lot of suffering most days. It's often very hard to not be consumed by these feelings. Sometimes the depressed person may reveal the anger they feel inwardly toward others who either seem to be having a carefree life (i.e., maybe envy is involved here) or because they often think others don't truly understand them. Good-hearted people often try to cheer up the depressed person; such comments may have good intensions ... but rarely are truly helpful. The depressed person hears those "Cheer up!" or "You don't have anything to be depressed about" messages as a reflection of how much others really don't understand their suffering. That can make the depressed person even more negative.

Another and possibly more frequent reason for saying mean things is that depression is often accompanied by irritability and low frustration tolerance. This may manifest in negative, angry, or hurtful comments, which can drive some people away (the resulting social isolation can intensify depression). Depressed people are much more likely to take things personally and to misunderstand some things others say. Family and friends of the depressed person need to appreciate that the anger and irritability are common symptoms of depression. Many people living with depression would never speak that way were they not depressed.

When It's Appropriate to Say What You Feel

It's totally appropriate to tell people you're having a tough day. It's very normal to need to talk to people about your sadness, worry, and fears about being depressed. The problem is when it goes on forever with little to no change on your part. The language you use when you're depressed affects your relationships, work, and life in general. Getting things done often starts by facing something with positive words, no matter how you feel. You'll see a big difference.

Here are some other thoughts to consider:

- When you meet someone new and they ask about your life, don't tell them your life story, especially what's wrong in your life. Give the person a positive version and then ask about their life.

- Know that you get one time to go on and on about how terrible things are and then you have to move on to what you're going to *do* about them.

- If someone asks how things are going and nothing's going well, say, "I'm hanging in there. What's new with you?"

- Always, always keep your mouth shut if all you can say is something mean or negative.

- What you say is who you are. Think of who you want to be and how you want to be seen, even when you're depressed. Use the language of that person, not the depressed you.

Remember: You are not a prerecorded doll with a string controlled by depression. You are 100 percent responsible for the words that come out of your mouth. They can make all the difference.

See a Therapist

Study after study shows that adding therapy to your depression treatment plan significantly decreases your depression symptoms. With the help of a qualified therapist, you can improve your ability to get things done.

You may already have a therapist and know the benefits, but if you feel sure therapy wouldn't work for you, please reconsider. Talking with someone about your problems might feel like an invasion of privacy, but taking a chance with someone new and even uncomfortable really can make a big difference in your productivity as well as your depression treatment overall.

Use Therapy to Help You Get Things Done

Finding a therapist who understands your needs when you're depressed is essential. If you want to go into your past and work on emotional issues, you can find a therapist who can help you do that. If you want to see a therapist for advice on how better to get moving with the things you want to do, it's important that you ask around and interview a therapist before you make an appointment. The relationship between a therapist and a client can be very powerful. Taking the time to find one who works for you can be of significant value to you.

Seeing a therapist is *not* a weakness. When you want or need support and to make changes, you don't have to do it all on your own. Seeking outside opinions and ideas from a professional who has worked with others like yourself can increase your ability to get things done much more quickly than if you have to discover everything for yourself.

Consider the following signs that therapy might be right for you:

- You find it difficult to get things done on your own.
- You know what you need to do but can't seem to implement the strategies due to negative and self-incriminating thoughts.
- You want an objective person to help you see the areas you need to change.

- You need someone to talk to about the feelings brought up when you feel you're not able to meet your potential.

- You're lonely and want human contact with someone who understands depression and has ideas about how to work on your loneliness.

It can be comforting to know that a therapist can help you with all this stuff. It's a lot easier than trying to handle the problems all on your own.

Rick's Story

I decided to go with a male therapist because I felt he would better understand what I go through as a father and as the person who goes to work every day. (My partner is home with our kids.) I don't tell people at work about my depression; I tell my therapist. I talk to him about my worries that this illness will be passed on to my kids. I worry that I'm setting a bad example by having days when I actually have to call in sick to take care of myself. I talk to my therapist about my inability to move up in the company like I want to. I can't take on as many clients as my co-workers do, and I see them get the promotions I want for myself. When I got my degree, I wanted to start my own business and have a lot of employees. But I have trouble doing what I do for my company; having my own company probably isn't in my future.

When my therapist hears my worries, he always points out the fact that I do a good job at work and am always praised. I've never had financial troubles because of the depression. My kids are fine, and my partner is understanding. He then reminds me that these worries often go away when the depression is not around, which is good because I can't see this on my own when I'm depressed. He is one of the most important people in my life because he listens without judging and then calmly points out what I can do to get through this.

My Story

I've been in therapy since age 19. Unfortunately, I've had many well-meaning therapists who wanted me to "explore my past" in detail to find out why staying in one job was so hard for me. They also wanted me to come up with a reason why I had trouble completing the projects I started with such enthusiasm. We looked at my family life, at my education, and at how I was raised to see what might have influenced my self-confidence.

There's no question this work helped me get to know myself better, but it never helped my productivity. The severity of the depression was missed for years because my personality is so out-going and rather excessive. When I started to look at my inability to work as a result of depression and not some personal failing, I found therapists who worked with me on getting around the depression in order to attack the real problem: my brain.

When I get really down on myself for not doing enough, Robin, my therapist of five years says, "Julie, you always asked me to remind you that this is a by-product of an illness. What can you do right now? Let's focus on that." She's right, and it takes her talking to me quite strongly to get through to my depressed brain. I often don't want to listen to her—rather, depression won't let me listen to her—but what she says always gets to me later. There are certainly days when I cry over my "lack of ability" to get things done, and she just listens. That helps as well.

What I do now:

- I see an action-oriented therapist who has a lot of ideas about how I can accept my situation and change what I can.

- I often go to my therapy session with a purpose.

- I remind my therapist to remind me that I'm depressed.

- I use therapy as a safe place to cry over what depression does to me.

- I listen to her insightful suggestions and use them.

Exercise

Finding an action-oriented therapist can be a challenge, so it's very important that you know what you need and want before you see someone. Look over the following list and check the therapy and therapist qualities you feel will help you the most.

I want a therapist who ...

☐ Helps me create a plan for getting through the workday.

☐ Doesn't mind if I cry, complain, and feel sorry for myself, as long as it's not the whole session.

☐ Uses *cognitive therapy* to help me realize my negative and often distorted thoughts about my lack of productivity.

☐ Helps me change my behaviors with a definite plan.

☐ Knows about depression and how it affects productivity.

When you determine the kind of therapist you seek, you can ask family, friends, and health-care professionals for referrals. It's very important that you see someone who works for you. You might have to try a few before finding someone who fits.

Cognitive therapy cuts through the fog of depression and makes you focus very specifically on what you think and say out loud. A trained therapist can listen to what you say, point out how it is possibly distorted, and offer you ways to change the language in order to change the thought behind the language. For example, you can change I never get anything done and never will to I've had trouble getting things done lately. This realistic appraisal of your current situation can give you a lot of hope for the future.

ASK DR. PRESTON

Q **Why does seeing a therapist often work better than asking friends and family for help?**

A Therapists who understand how to treat depression successfully know the right questions to ask. They realize that responses such as "Snap out of it" or "It'll be better soon" aren't helpful. They appreciate the need to discuss some feelings and life events over and over again. They know about specific techniques and homework assignments that can help combat depression, and they know about adjunct treatments such as antidepressants and bright-light therapy. And finally, because they're not your friends or family, they can maintain a more realistic perspective.

Don't Fear Therapy

Seeing a therapist is a sign of strength when faced with depression.

Here are some other thoughts to consider:

- Research different styles of therapy, including cognitive therapy that teaches awareness of how what you say and do determines your mood; behavioral therapy that helps you look at the behaviors that lead to more depression so that you can replace them with more constructive behaviors; and interpersonal therapy where you examine what current problematic relationships may be contributing to depression and then learn strategies for more effective communication and problem solving in important relationships. Finding a therapist who uses a combination of the above techniques is often a great help. When you make a decision, you can ask for referrals and make calls.

- You don't have to want to do the busy work of finding a therapist. It may be overwhelming. But if your goal is to have a supportive therapist who can help you get things done and feel good about yourself, you have to take the first uncomfortable step. It can take less than a few hours for possible years of benefit.

- Listen to yourself and not the others who may say that therapy isn't what you need.

- Knowing you have someone who will listen to you without judgment can be a tremendous help for depression.

- Action-oriented therapists can have a lot of good advice on how to make the life choices that help you focus on what you can do. Then they can give you practical advice on how to get moving and get things done.

Remember: Most people take more time picking fruit in a grocery store than they do choosing a therapist. Find someone who works for *you.* The legwork you do up front will pay off down the road.

Accept the Limitations Caused by Depression

At one time or another, everyone with depression has dreams of what they could do *if only* they weren't depressed. Facing the reality of what you can do might feel devastating if you've had a dream, possibly since childhood, of how you want to work or where you want to be by a certain point in your life. For many people, it's the 30-year mark. You think, *I should have reached my goals by 30! Other people are a lot farther than I am by now!* This might be true, but it's probably also true that they don't deal with depression.

Acceptance Means Not Giving Up

There's nothing wrong with grand dreams and goals; they are an essential part of life. But when you're depressed, you might have to evaluate your dreams and goals and change them if they're not realistic for you now. Compare what you think you should and could do if you didn't have depression with what you can realistically do when you're depressed. This assessment naturally depends on the depth and length of your depression, but it's necessary.

When you have a project due at work or an event to plan, there's no point in constantly trying to do it in a way you've never been able to do in the past. Accepting that you have limits, and learning to work within those limits, improves your quality of work as well as your mood.

Are any of the following signs that it's time for acceptance applicable to you?

- You consistently say, "I would … if I didn't have depression."
- You continually hope for change in areas that might not realistically change.
- People in your life say you're not meeting your potential, but you know you're doing your best.

- Your goals and dreams don't take depression into account.

- You measure your current situation by what you could or *should* do instead of what you're actually doing well.

It's easy to *think* of what can't be done. There's no action in that, and the thinking can go on forever! Acting with an awareness of what you *can* do gets things done.

John's Story

When I talk about my limitations to friends, they say, "Oh, John. You don't know what it might be like in the future!" I want to say, "Well, I'm fifty-six years old. Unless there's some amazing break-through I've not heard about, I think I'm pretty realistic about what I can and can't do." They then say, "But John! Don't give up hope! You just don't know how it will be ten years from now!"

I wish they could change places with me just for one week of depression. I know what they say is said out of kindness. It's hard to be with someone who has a chronic illness, and they worry about me, especially when I have to go to the hospital. My friends want me to get better. I want to get better, too. But the reality is that management is all I can do. I *manage* depression. I no longer believe it's magically going to end one day. I've looked at what I can and can't do. I see reality. I don't like it, but I have mostly accepted it. This doesn't mean I don't keep trying 100 percent to get better. I just don't hold my breath that a miracle is coming.

The miracle is that since accepting things, my life is *so* much better. I don't try to do what I can't, and I focus on doing a really great job at what I can do. I feel a lot more comfortable in my life now.

My Story

A psychologist friend of mine once said to me, "You're extremely attached to defending your inability." At first I thought, *Wow, that's a tough thing to say to someone who's depressed and has been depressed for most of her life!* I wanted to say, "You don't understand what I go through and what depression has taken from my life!" But within a few minutes, I saw that I was doing exactly what he said I was doing.

I've spent the past 20 years defining myself by what I can't do. If only I didn't have depression, I'd be running a huge company by now. I'd be able to sing professionally on Broadway! I could handle full-time work. I could be a star! I could write a book every three months! Maybe this would be the case if I didn't have depression. But that's never happened, has it? No. My friend is right. I never focus on what I can do. It's never enough. I rarely say to myself, *Wow, Julie, look how much you get done despite the depression! Look, Julie, you wrote books, didn't you? Yes, you started at age 39 and you missed all of those productive years, but look where you are now compared to just 10 years ago.* Even as I write this, I think of what could have been or could be if only this illness would go away forever. It's true. I'm very, very attached to defending what I can't do instead of accepting what I can do. I have severe limitations due to depression. I have a disability. Those are the facts. How long am I going to fight this and talk of what life could be like? If only, if only, if only …. That's no way to live life, and I want to stop it.

What I do now (or at least try hard to do now!):

- I face the fact that I've *never* been able to work full-time in an office for more than a year without getting sick, and probably won't be able to in the future.

- I focus on what I *can* do. I even make a list of what I can do and add to it when I get something new done.

- I make sure I have challenging people in my life who will tell me the truth, even when it's hard for me to hear. This is especially true for my therapist.

- I accept that I often have weeks and even months where it's very, very hard to work to my realistic capacity.

- I go on no matter what, even when these limitations make me cry.

Exercise

This is a hard exercise to do; the length of your depression will affect your answers. When you look over your life, what have you had trouble doing because of depression? If your depression is recent, what changes have you seen since you've been depressed?

Work _____

_____

_____

Taking care of yourself _____

_____

_____

Family _____

_____

_____

Travel _____

_____

_____

Dreams/goals _____

_____

_____

Artistic pursuits _____

_____

_____

Now, each time the *I wish, I should,* or *if only* comes up, answer with this:

I may not be able to do _____, but I can do _____!

Accepting limitations, especially those that significantly influenced your past, hurts. But remember, you're reading this book, which means you can change and get better every day.

Ask Dr. Preston

Q **Do you think it's giving up if a person accepts that they have limitations from depression and that they will have to change their life accordingly?**

I wouldn't frame it as "giving up" but more in terms of acceptance. However, many depressive-fueled conclusions *are* distorted and unrealistic. It's important to know that depression can make you feel that you have serious limitations, even though that's false most of the time. Only access your limitations when you're more stable. When you're at that point, you have to recognize that because of experiences you can't control, your nervous system isn't good at regulating your moods, and being self-critical about this never helps. Knowing these brain-caused limitations helps you make decisions that can lead to successfully getting things done versus continually trying tasks that only frustrate and make you further depressed.

What's Real for You?

What do you say to yourself about your limitations? Can you accept them and then focus on what you *can* do? It may be that your depression is new and will end in a short period of time. The good news is that your limitations will probably end soon, too. Or you might have chronic depression and your limitations have been present for all your adult life. Whatever the case, assess where you are now. Then face it and move on.

Here are some other thoughts to consider:

- Look at what dreams you're still searching for and see if they're possible or if they're unrealistic in terms of how they will affect your mood.

- Don't give up, but don't drive yourself to do something you've never been able to do without getting depressed.

- Depression is an illness. If you have diabetes, the desire to become a cake decorator might not be a realistic choice. Likewise, there might be some things you can't do when you're depressed.

- Everyone has limitations. You have to know your own and then move on.

Remember: Depression might limit your ability to get things done the way you want to. Once you know what your limitations are, you can accept them and focus on what you *can* do.

Explore Medication

It cannot be stressed enough that depression is often a serious physiological illness that can benefit greatly from the use of medications. Treating chronic depression without medications is possible, but statistically, those who use antidepressants, anxiety medications, and/or attention-deficit hyperactivity disorder (ADHD) medications to treat the illness can lead a more productive life.

Medications Change the Brain

As you may know, the depressed brain has chemical "issues." When medications work effectively, they can help return those wayward chemicals to better working order. Just like an engine tune-up for your car, medications can help your brain work more smoothly. A smoothly operating brain operates as a catalyst to getting things done, as opposed to an ill brain that creates a barrier and makes your life so much more difficult.

Medications for depression can change lives. They're not a crutch, and although for some people they only take care of part of the symptoms, they're a huge foundation for treating depression so you can finish projects. If your depression is mild or you're satisfied with the way you manage depression now, using the strategies in this book along with other changes might work fine for you. But if you've tried everything you can and your depression still negatively affects your life and your productivity, exploring medication is a very good and very smart idea.

Consider some of these signs that medications could help you:

- You've worked for more than six months to manage your depression and it's not really getting better.

- You see depression as a physical illness.

- You've experienced depression for a large part of your life.

- Your work and family life are suffering because of your depression.

- People in your life are asking you to try medications, and you can tell that they're truly concerned.

Ask yourself, *Would medications help me right now? If so, what is my next step?*

Peter's Story

My family has always called me lazy, as well as a few other things. Here are some of my past labels: you … don't want to work, are on drugs, are doomed to failure, are unmotivated. I look back on my life, and I see an unfinished college degree as well as jobs started with a lot of enthusiasm that quickly faded. No ability to finish a project. It's like everything just sort of deflated after a few months. I had trouble making money. I can remember thinking that I didn't want to live like this. I wanted to start my own graphic design business—I'm really good at it—but it just seemed impossible. I'd get the business license and then stop. I'd then get some enthusiasm and do some research and then stop. I felt absolutely miserable. I wanted this business, yet I was such a mess I couldn't even do the simple stuff needed to get it started.

I finally listened to a friend and went to see a doctor about my depression. She put me on an antidepressant, but it didn't work. We tried another and it started to work on my moods, but I still had trouble with my work life. Then we talked about an ADHD drug. I've never thought of myself as ADHD at all. I wasn't like that as a kid, but as an adult, I had a lot of the signs of ADHD. When I started the ADHD drug along with the antidepressant, my life changed 100 percent. For the first time in my life I was able to think of a project, create a plan, and finish it. I'm 39 years old. Better late than never.

My Story

So many people think taking medications for depression is weak. I wonder why that is? I had a roommate in the 1980s who told me she was taking meds for depression. I said what so many people have said to me: "Why do you need to do that? I know many people who are a lot sicker than you are. You should be able to take care of this yourself." I wish I could find her now. I'm mortified at what I said, especially because the years after I lived with her were basically terrible for me with depression. I now see her as a success; I hope she is.

Too many people think antidepressants are just "happy pills" and that people who take them are just looking for a way out of their problems. I've had people say to me, "Medications change who you are. I don't want to lose my personality." I always reply, "The right medications actually deal with the illness that keeps you from being who you really are. Getting help with depression from meds is a way to live the life you want to live." Some listen, some don't. I know that those who do try medications tell me they can work so much better than they used to. For many people, medications save lives and work like a "miracle."

The medication I take for depression works on about 25 percent of my depression symptoms, depending on the stressors in my life. But the medication really, really helps my concentration and anxiety, which is a big, big help. I wish I could get more relief from the depression itself, but I'll take what I can get. I waited six months for the side effects to calm down, but they did. I think a *lot* more clearly now. When I combine medications with the strategies in this book, I can complete projects for the first time in my life.

What I do now:

- I take my medication every day. In fact, I'm afraid to miss a day.

- I add an antianxiety medication when I need it.

- I always look for another medication that may work with or work better than what I'm taking.

- I will never give up on medications.

- I'm aware that my depression medication actually helps in many other areas of my life and well-being, including psychosis, concentration, sleep, and anxiety. In reality, the medication helps more in these areas than in actual depression relief!

Exercise

Complete these sentences:

The thought of taking medications makes me feel _____.

My family thinks _____.

I should be able to _____ on my own.

Medications are _____ *(expensive, dangerous, numbing ...).*

Then look at the following information and see if any of it changes your mind:

- Recent research from a National Institute of Mental Health study shows that up to 70 percent of people with depression can significantly reduce depression symptoms when they find the right combination of medications.

- A comprehensive treatment plan that includes strategies such as the ones in this book, lifestyle changes, therapy, and anti-depressant treatment can help the majority of people with depression reduce and even completely eliminate their depression symptoms.

- Newer antidepressants have significantly fewer side effects than those in the past.

Knowledge is power! If you think medications could ease some of your pain and help you become more productive, talk to an experienced health-care professional about your options.

ASK DR. PRESTON

Q Why are so many people against depression medications?

A Many misperceptions and misunderstandings surround the role of medications. You might think that many of the medications used to treat depression are habit forming. Or maybe you think that they are a crutch and that you need to deal with your "problems" on your own. Both are untrue.

Or maybe others' opinions are causing the hesitation. You might hear, "You don't need drugs. Look at me—I deal with things and you need to do the same" or "Just deal with it." And the very common, "You need to try harder." The people who say these things have a lack of knowledge of depression and often don't even know how the medications can work.

Plus, the extensive media coverage given to antidepressants over that past few years regarding the risk of suicide in adolescents can be overwhelming. The concerns are real, but they also must be taken into context. Many people who take antidepressants with the help of a skilled health-care professional do so successfully.

Try Something New

It's very difficult to treat some depressions without medications. If you feel that medications are right for you, work with a health-care professional to find the right medications for you. This can take up to a year sometimes, so don't give up, and remember that side effects can go away if you give them time. Do all that you can medically to take care of depression so you can then use the strategies in this book to help you increase your productivity even more.

Here are some other thoughts to consider:

- Be assured that antidepressants are not habit forming. You are very unlikely to become addicted to antidepressants.

- Know that the media coverage that focuses on the potential suicidal thoughts caused by medications are a real concern, but these are rare side effects for most medications. Educate yourself, and make an informed decision.

- Yes, pharmaceutical companies make a huge amount of money off antidepressants, but that's no reason to deny yourself a potentially life-changing medication.

- There's very little chance that antidepressants will "change who you are." In reality, it's depression that changes who you are. These drugs are designed to help you maintain the real you and all your potential.

- If a doctor or therapist wants you to try medications, that's not an indication that they don't want to listen to you anymore. It usually means they want to help ease your suffering so you can more effectively work together.

Remember: Medications that successfully treat depression can take away many of the problems you have with getting things done.

Find Your Work Purpose

Depression takes away the feeling that what you do has purpose; it's one of the most debilitating symptoms of the illness. If getting things done gives you no pleasure or sense of accomplishment, then what's the point of doing anything? For some, a sense of duty keeps them going. For others, it's money. For many, it's a family obligation. Unfortunately, this doesn't mean you feel good about what you do.

Your Work Does Have Purpose

If you seek to find purpose in your current work and obligations, you can see immediate improvements. What you do *does* have meaning, because it's how you make money, support the people you love, get out of the house, and improve your life. It might not be the work you want to do at this moment, but it has purpose. You just have to find it.

When you discover the purpose in what you're doing now, you can then think of what you really want to be doing. What makes you happy? What makes you feel like you're making a difference in the world? People who deal with depression need to be sure that what they do on a daily basis has a strong meaning.

Do any of these signs indicating you need to find work that feels more purposeful to you ring true?

- Your job isn't satisfying.

- You don't look forward to work even when you're not depressed.

- Your work isn't challenging enough.

- You simply don't know what to do careerwise.

- Even though you love them very much, staying at home with your children is not what you thought it would be.

- You want to stay focused on the positives of what your work offers even when the depression makes it difficult.

Cheryl's Story

My work is work. I do it because I have to. I always do it to my best ability and know that others are fine with my work. I never thought being a receptionist would work for me, but I really do need something where I don't have to take extra work and worries home with me. It's a pretty good career, but I'm not excited about it.

What excites me is horses. I volunteer with a nonprofit organization that uses horses to help disabled kids. And I love it. I love it less on the days I'm depressed, but I never cancel. I go because it makes me feel like I'm making a difference. I don't say, "These kids are worse off than me. I have no reason to be so depressed." Instead I say, "I use their love and enthusiasm to help myself function. We both have our challenges." I often have the thought that I could do this work full-time. I'm working on that.

My Story

I know what I write helps others. People write me and tell me so. But I don't have daily contact with my readers, so the impact isn't easy for me to see. I do know that it helps me to have a goal and reach it. But purpose has often eluded me. I've constantly searched for something that will give me the feeling that I'm living life and doing things that make a difference.

Then something amazing happened. I started to teach writing classes. I can literally watch students go from idea to finished project. I can help *them* reach their goals. I can see their excitement and feed off it. I found a purpose in helping others find their purpose. I've always loved teaching but didn't feel I could do it professionally due to my limitations. (There I go again, defending my inability!) No, I can't be a college professor. That hurts, but I can do my best. I teach a night class at a local community college, and it makes me feel good!

What I do now:

- I work hard to not worry so much about how my students are feeling toward me. This leads to less stress and less depression.

- I focus on what I can do instead of expecting myself to be perfect.

- I look for a purpose in the moment. When I'm sitting in front of my computer writing and I have the thought that my life is empty, I remind myself, *No, it's not. What I do has purpose. I'm writing a book right now, and that's my purpose.*

- I know my writing makes a difference. I know I help people. I know this, and I have to focus on it when I write.

Exercise

It's important that you rationally look at what you do now and how it impacts your life and the lives of others. List three ways your current work has purpose:

1. _____
2. _____
3. _____

List three ways that the way you take care of your family has purpose:

1. _____
2. _____
3. _____

List five ways your work affects others:

1. _____
2. _____
3. _____
4. _____
5. _____

Look over the following list and decide what suggestions or type of work would really help you find your higher purpose:

- ☐ Ask for a different position at work
- ☐ Train others at work
- ☐ Change your work
- ☐ Travel
- ☐ Explore the creative arts
- ☐ Uplift the world
- ☐ Get a college degree

- [ ] Volunteer
- [ ] Go back to work
- [ ] Mentor
- [ ] Quit work and stay home with your kids
- [ ] Quit your job for something more purposeful
- [ ] Teach
- [ ] Work in a religious/spiritual setting
- [ ] Work with animals
- [ ] Work with kids
- [ ] Work with the disabled
- [ ] Work with your hands

If you're not able to do what you love in your current work, explore taking a class, teaching a class, or volunteering until you can either make changes within your current work or try something completely new.

ASK DR. PRESTON

Q **How do you find purpose when one of the main symptoms of depression is a feeling that life has no purpose?**

A It's very important to take a realistic look at your life, first of all. When you ask a depressed person what they do that's meaningful, 90 percent of the time they'll say "nothing." But careful reflection on this, often with the help of a significant other or therapist, can help you identify things you're currently doing or have done in the past that do have purpose and meaning. It's all about wading through the depression to get to the reality of the purpose your life already has. When you do this, if you truly find that your life lacks purpose, you can work from a stable and rational place to do something about it.

Your Purpose Might Surprise You

Maybe you can find purpose within a small part of your work. Is there something you do that you especially enjoy? Can you ask for more of that work and pass off the other work to someone who likes what you don't? Examine what you really want and find a way to do it. The stronger your purpose, the more power you have over depression.

Here are some other thoughts to consider:

- Ask the people in your life to tell you what they see as your purpose. And listen to them!

- Get out a piece of paper and list all the things that give you purpose, from family, friends, work, creating something, and volunteering to spiritual practices and maintaining your physical health. Even if this is hard, do it! Then put the list up on your wall so you can see it when you wake up in the morning.

- Live each day with a goal of looking at what you do that makes a difference.

- Look for purpose in the everyday world instead of thinking that your life has no meaning.

- Start small if you want to make changes.

Remember: Finding a purpose lessens your depression symptoms significantly. If you're not sure of what your purpose is, start exploring today. Then go for it!

Be Realistic About the Hours in a Week

There are only so many hours in a week; that's a fact you can't get around, no matter how long your to-do (or *should*-do) list is. People *without* depression are often pressed for time. But when you have the added pressure of managing depression, your week can be even more stressful. Overscheduling when you're depressed can be disastrous and could shut you down completely.

Where Does the Time Go?

There are 168 hours in a week. On average, most people sleep 7 hours a night. Add to that 1 hour to each day for getting ready in the morning and then again for bed, and that's 56 hours. 112 hours left. If you work outside the home, factor in commuting, lunch, and work hours, probably on the low side of 45 hours a week; you might also have to add business dinners, networking, or travel to this time. Assume the same for someone who is home with small children. This leaves 67 hours for outside obligations. Now assume 3 hours a day at least for eating and taking care of other personal needs, for a total of 21 hours. This leaves 46 hours. If you take care of children, you can add at least 2 hours a day devoted to your children. That's 14 hours. This leaves a total of 32 hours. If you don't have kids, it may be that those 2 hours a day are taken up by either television, seeing friends, or reading. If you exercise, you can assume at least 4 hours a week, which means 14 hours are left. For those who are overscheduled or those who work or go to school, this can be many more hours. Evening obligations can take up to an hour a day, as can yard work and house management, including bills. Talking on the phone is another time drainer. This leaves 4 hours a day for your other needs.

Where's the time for you? Or alone time with a partner? Running errands, seeing friends, going to movies, art, going to the doctor, or trips to the bank? If you work more than 40 hours a week, you can see how this time can easily dwindle to 0. No wonder a depressed person wants to shut down! There can be little time for self-rejuvenation.

Do any of these signs that you might need to keep better track of your time sound familiar to you?

- Even when your mood is low, you keep on a schedule that's not healthy for you.
- You do more because you feel guilty about not being able to do enough.
- You work more than 50 hours a week.
- You sleep all day and then don't have time to get anything done.

People often focus on how much time they have on a specific day instead of planning ahead for a week's worth of hours. If this is the case for you, it may be that you're being too hard on yourself for not getting things done when the real problem is simply not having enough time!

Adam's Story

How am I supposed to get all the things I need to get done with such limited time? I think this is why I literally shut down when I'm depressed. All I want to do is get into bed and pull the covers over my head, but if I actually do this (I used to do it a lot), then I feel even more overwhelmed and things keep piling up.

When I really looked at the hours I have to work, take care of my kids, and take care of my basic needs, I just felt so much relief. I thought it was a lack of time management on my part. But now I know that time is limited and there's only so much I can do. Period. It was a tough adjustment, but I now use an hourly planner, and I look at it a lot. It really makes a difference.

My Story

I tend to overbook myself when I'm depressed. It's actually good for me, but there are limits. When I plan to do two things on one night a few hours apart, or if I have five phone calls to return in a day, I can't get it all done. Depression is so darn sneaky. On the days that I'm lonely and the hours loom in front of me, the depression says, "See, Julie. No one wants to be with you." Then the phone will start ringing and I'll make plans and the depression says, "You're doing too much, Julie. You don't have time for this!" I can never win with that logic.

What I do now:

- I make myself go to the library to write for three or four hours every day. This is realistic.

- Then I have to figure out how many more hours I have. Will I see my nephew? Then I can't do happy hour with a friend. Do I want to watch *American Idol* with my mom? The choices are endless, and I often overbook. I now think before I say yes to doing something.

- I sometimes say yes to things without thinking at all how many hours I have and how many hours it will take. I'm just so happy to be out and doing something.

- I know I don't need to be alone and I don't watch television very often, so I do have more hours to be with people.

- I accept that despite using my strategies, there are days when I waste hours and hours because I'm depressed. It's a lot better than it used to be, and I'm going to make sure it gets better in the future.

Maybe you have to stop and face reality. If you're depressed and it's not getting better, you might be doing so much that your brain can't keep up.

Exercise

There are 168 hours in a week. How many hours do you …

Sleep? _____

Commute? _____

Spend on your kids' activities? _____

Work? _____

Watch television? _____

Travel? _____

Socialize? _____

Lose to depression, on average? _____

Total _____

Subtract your total from 168, the hours in a week. How much time is left for you?

ASK DR. PRESTON

Q **Why is it so hard to see what you actually can do in a week?**

A When you're depressed, you usually aren't as productive or efficient as when you're well. You don't use your time effectively and you waste a lot of time. This can lead to feelings of even lower self-worth. Plus, people with agitated depression can take on too much with the same result as those who can't work well at all.

There Are Only So Many Hours

Time may be relative, but it's finite when it comes to your day. It doesn't bend or give you a break. If you're not getting enough sleep, getting things done, or living the life you want, you might be trying to squeeze 30 hours of work into a 24-hour day.

Here are some other thoughts to consider:

- The hours you have for free time are precious. Don't let depression waste them away. Do what you would do if you weren't depressed. It's better than sitting in front of a bad sitcom drinking a beer.

- Is it realistic for you to take on that job as a Boy Scout leader? PTA volunteer? Church caregiver?

- If you run out of time to get all things done by the end of every day, something has to go.

- If you need alone time, schedule it in.

- Twenty-four hours is twenty-four hours. You need sleep, and you need time to do all the little things life requires. Try to have two to three unscheduled hours a day. It might feel impossible, but it can be done.

Remember: Create a schedule that helps you manage depression so you can get things done—realistically during the time you have each week.

Allow Time for Positive Results

These are the days of fast food, instant downloadable music, and love at first sight (or so the movies want us to believe). But when you want to make changes to lessen your depression and increase your productivity, time can feel like your archenemy. Often, when you make a positive change your depression eases, but the big changes may take quite a bit longer. In fact, you'll probably have to go through a lot of trial and error to find what strategies work for you.

Positive Results Depend on Your Situation

If your depression is a result of a certain situation in your life such as the wrong job, a troublesome child, or a bad romantic relationship, making some big changes in the troublesome area can likely produce very quick mood changes in a positive way. But for those who deal with a more chronic depression that seems to just hang around no matter what they try, change will have many steps and setbacks. This can lead to frustration and possibly giving up before they have a chance to get better.

Unfortunately, many changes don't give a reward or even a great feeling right in the moment. It can often take time for the rewards to build. For example, saying no might be so uncomfortable for you that you don't see the point. Asking your family to do things around the house might cause such chaos—especially if they're used to you doing everything—it can feel easier just to maintain the status quo. Dealing with a difficult co-worker, a child's angry basketball coach, or a boss who keeps piling on the work can feel unbearable. But most change is like this. You have to get past the unpleasant feelings to get to the good ones. You have to give yourself time to get better.

Do you see in yourself any of these signs of impatience?

- You feel that your family will never understand what you need.
- Your depression doesn't seem to respond to anything so you keep walking into situations that actually make the depression worse.

- You don't like to wait for anything.
- Your depression thoughts telling you things are not going quickly enough are stronger than your realistic thoughts.

Using the strategies in this book to get things done might produce results more quickly than you think. On the other hand, some strategies might take a long time to result in more productivity. Expect both.

Margaret's Story

I stopped caffeine, started walking, and tried to keep away from the people who make me stressed and nervous. After two months of craving coffee and dealing with the nonstop arguments in my family, I saw little change in the depression except that I slept better at night. So I went back to coffee, started yelling at my brother again, and missed my walking days.

What a disaster! I never realized that my new regime was actually helping my anxiety and my attitude so much. I just didn't see it. In reality, it was a relief to sleep better. The changes really were making a difference. So I started them again.

My Story

I started to manage my depression eight years ago. It took a few years for me to figure out what worked and what didn't to manage my symptoms. And it took my family many years to understand what I was doing and why I needed their help and understanding. I'm glad I didn't know how long all this would take or I really would have been discouraged!

Eight years later, I still face the same challenges. But the difference is that I use my strategies to make the most of my time when I'm depressed. I know I'll do this the rest of my life. I truly believe that I'll only get better at management as time goes on. If I focus on immediate results, I'm often disappointed.

Depression is serious and involves my brain. It's not simply an emotional issue caused by something in my life. If that were the case, I could make some quick changes and definitely get positive results much more quickly. When a person stops cigarettes or decides to lose weight and sticks to it, those results can be fast and immediately feel worth it. Knowing that I have the rest of my life to deal with the depression reminds me that the results of positive change may take a lot longer than I want them to. When I stopped eating what I call junk-food sugar almost a year ago, I expected my moods to get immediately better. They didn't. But my body changed, and that made me feel better about myself. I had more fun with my clothes and going out with friends. This helped my depression.

What I do now:

- I try to think in years instead of months when waiting for results of something I change.

- I know that getting upset and impatient at how long something takes such as working on relationship problems that affect my depression will only make things worse.

- I always remind myself that the time passes anyway. I can choose to work daily on my health and wait for the long-term results, or I can do nothing and have the time pass anyway with no results at all.

Exercise

For some reason, we tend to forget the tremendous amount of work we put into our daily tasks and abilities simply because they're so common and expected. Think about it. How long did you practice walking until you were able to do it with ease? How long did it take you to learn to ride a bike? How long did you practice before you could drive?

Now, how long will it take you to implement the strategies in this book? Do you feel you'll see results in one week? Six months? A year? Where do you want to be in five years regarding your productivity?

Give the strategies in this book at least three months to see results. Even the small results can keep you going. If you're only looking for the big changes in an unrealistic amount of time, you will surely get frustrated.

ASK DR. PRESTON

Q **Why are people with depression so much more likely to give up before they see any results?**

A Depression brings with it powerful and pervasive effects of negative thinking that color all perceptions and predictions for the future. Hand in hand with that is impatience and low tolerance for frustration.

For most of us, large tasks like completing a significant work project or finishing a college course require a considerable amount of stick-to-itiveness and what psychologists call "delay of gratification." A lot of what enables the nondepressed person to persevere is being able to keep the long-range goals and anticipated positive outcomes in mind. Neurochemical changes in the brain (primarily decreased metabolic activity in the prefrontal lobes) make such delay of gratification as well as the ability to accurately project into the future very difficult for those who are depressed. This, added to generally negative evaluations, makes it tremendously hard to fight off the impatience. Breaking expectations into small sections can help you to see that progress *is* being accomplished.

Time Changes Everything

It's true that time marches on no matter what you do. So why not make the time matter? Why just let that time pass without making positive changes? The decision may be instant, but the results can be a long time coming. That's okay. When things are going slowly and you think you'll never be able to get things done and improve your life, remind yourself that this isn't true; it's just taking a lot longer than you want or expect. Be patient and think in the long term. It's worth the wait.

Here are some other thoughts to consider:

- Set goals and then double the time you originally chose to get them done.

- When you feel hopeless and that things will never get better, always remind yourself that if you just keep working at it, things will definitely change. Don't let depression convince you they won't.

- Give yourself a year to learn to truly get things done when you're depressed, without having to think of each strategy constantly.

- See your depression management as a process, not a destination. You can still have the goal of ridding depression from your life— that's very possible and many people do it! But until you reach that point, you're on a journey, not in a race.

Remember: The strategies in this book are lifelong. As you try each one, ask yourself, *What is the* realistic *time frame to see results?*

Create Creativity

Sadly, artistic creativity is one of the first things to go when you get depressed. It's as though your eye for color and design disappear. Ideas dry up, and your usually active and creative mind becomes static. This is especially hard to deal with if your livelihood is in the arts or your job requires new and creative ideas on a regular basis.

You *Can* Create When You're Depressed

A depressed mind often forgets the motions of creativity. Getting things done in terms of the practical parts of life is difficult enough, but when it comes to creating art, you can feel especially depressed. It's one thing not to be able to do your bills; it's very different when you can't create something beautiful that enhances your life in so many ways.

But just because the desire to do something when you're depressed is gone, it doesn't mean your ability to actually create is gone as well. The ability is still there. Your memory of art and your skill don't go away. Reaching that creative place just isn't as easy as you want it to be.

But you have to find it. You have to dust it off and use it like you usually do. You can even use your depression as an artistic tool. What you create might really surprise you.

Do any of these signs indicating you need to resurrect your creativity ring true for you?

- Your ideas feel dried up.
- You haven't drawn, used color, thought of new projects, or worked with your hands for too long.
- You feel like your talent will be gone forever.
- You've forgotten how good it feels to create once you get started.
- You're waiting to feel like creating something instead of just doing it.

If you remind yourself over and over that you don't have to feel a strong creative spark to create, you can start to produce again.

Armand's Story

I'm very creative when I'm well. I usually have to choose between all the projects I want to do. When I get depressed, I stop creating. I don't get out my paints. I don't make the comics I love to story-board. I stop drawing in my idea notebook. Everything stops.

Sometimes I don't even realize it's happening until my partner asks, "Why aren't you painting?" I answer, "I just don't feel like it these days. I can't think of what to do." She knows this means I'm depressed, and she knows what she has to do. She gets out my paints and literally says, "You *know* painting makes you feel better and not painting makes you feel terrible. You don't have to come up with something new right now. You can just copy something or work on an old idea. You expect too much of yourself anyway. Just make something!"

I feel so much resistance when I see the paints. I'm sure nothing will come out of me. But it always does. My subject matter may be darker, but that's okay. Art changes with moods anyway, and I know that just doing it is what matters, not how easy it feels or how it looks. It's the process of using my hands and getting something on paper that's important.

My Story

I had a very serious depression last year when I had trouble with my publisher over a project that we couldn't get to work. I ended up working for free for five months. This crushed me. I did what I always do and just kept going; but looking back, I see that something changed at that time but I just assumed I was burned out on writing and needed a break.

A few months ago my therapist said, "Julie, I've really noticed that you're not as creative as you used to be." At first I thought she was crazy. I'd been writing and was getting projects to publishers, but I realized she was right—I was basically completing old ideas.

She then said, "You used to constantly bring in new projects to show me. All the book ideas and ways of managing your depression. You used your colored pens and made charts and mind maps, and I could tell how happy that made you." She was right. My ideas had dried up. My pens that I usually loved so much actually upset me. The big pads of paper I usually carried around with me were on my bookshelf. How did this happen? For the first time in the five years since using the strategies I write about in this book, I stopped doing something I loved so much: creating treatment plans and book ideas.

I thought a lot about what she said and realized I had to find the old me. I missed my passion for ideas. Sometimes it takes a person on the outside to point out that you've stopped doing something you love.

What I do now:

- I got out one of my big pads of paper and made a mind map of all my current ideas. They were in there; I just had to force them out.

- I printed a sign that said, "I can create creativity!" and put it on my desk.

- I talked about this with a friend of mine who also has a lot of depression. She said she was having the same problem and didn't know what to do about it. So we decided to do a project together.

Exercise

What do you like to do creatively? Photography? Drawing? Gardening? Singing? Writing? Working with clay? Music? Coming up with new advertising ideas? Writing teaching plans? New building designs?

Now, what have you stopped doing because of depression? Write it here:

_____

_____

_____

What are you going to do about it?

- ☐ Take a class.
- ☐ Teach someone else what you love to do.
- ☐ Work with a friend.
- ☐ Tell yourself you'll just create for one hour and see what happens.
- ☐ Do half!
- ☐ Get out something old and use it for inspiration.

Artists can't always be super-creative. Writers can't always write with ease. This is especially important to remember when you're dealing with depression and want to express yourself creatively.

Ask Dr. Preston

Q **Do you think it's possible to make yourself be creative when you're depressed?**

A Creativity is often significantly shut down with depression, along with other kinds of cognitive processes. Creativity is not just thinking in clever ways; it's also having emotionally charged thoughts. These creative thoughts are felt as enthusiasm or excitement and often become blunted during depression. That's why the *desire* for creativity is absent. You can get past this by sitting down and doing what you used to do. This can often spark a creative thought, and the process can move forward.

Some writers, poets, and artists express their feeling through their work and may capture the essence of how they're feeling. The act of writing or painting in itself can help some people when they're depressed. Creativity can be a way of self-expression or a way to become clearer about the issues that are troubling them.

Don't Wait to Create

Create, create, and create some more. Use color in a new way. Take a picture from a different point of view. Write in a different genre. Compose music that represents your mood. You don't have to feel well to do some beautiful work. Depression makes you feel that you're artistically limited, but you're not.

Here are some other thoughts to consider:

- Think of the supplies you use to create your artwork. Put them on a table and look at them. They are your friends, not a sign that you can't create anymore.

- Don't think of how it used to be. Think of what you can do now, and create something that comes from this moment.

- Create something that shows what it's like to be depressed, a snapshot of where you are now. If you cry on the art, that's just a part of where you are now.

- Expect resistance from depression. It hates creativity for some reason. You need to break the hold depression has on your creativity by making something tangible, so you can see the results of your work.

- Think of how you feel in the middle of doing something creative instead of how hard it is to start.

Remember: Don't wait until to feel better! Create something now! When you're better and you look at the work, you'll see that you are just as creative as always.

PS: I had no desire to write today. I'm depressed and felt scattered and uncreative. So I wrote about not being able to write. This is the result, and I think it's pretty good! What are you going to create today?

Praise Yourself All Day

When you're depressed, it can feel impossible to find the words you need to praise yourself. The personal and negative depression onslaught you face is often very hard to fight. And even if you only slightly believe what the depression says, you still get in a cycle of doing what needs to get done and then having your efforts shot down by the negative words of depression. Self-praise can be hard even for people who don't have depression, so go easy on yourself if the words don't come easily for you when you're having a tough day.

Take Back the Real You

The real you, outside of depression, probably likes you a lot and wants you to do well. If you think rationally about the thoughts you have when you're depressed, it's easy to see that they're often ludicrous and so unrealistic that you could laugh at them if they weren't so painful: *You will never be a success. You are a* terrible *parent. Your art is* worthless. You would (hopefully!) never talk to another person this way, so don't let depression talk to you this way, either.

Nothing is as black and white as depression makes it seem. Ever. You have to start exercising your self-praising ability. It's probably very rusty at this point, but you can change that, no matter how long depression has said terrible things about you. Remember this and praise yourself all day, even if the best you can do is to get up from a chair and make lunch. Saying "Good for me! I did it!" will become natural over time, and you might find that eventually self-praise pops out when you least expect it!

Consider the following signs you need to take over and praise yourself:

- You hear only negative thoughts about yourself.
- You are being very cruel to yourself.
- It feels impossible to think positively.

- Praise was not emphasized in your family, so you don't have the language to counteract the negative thoughts.

- You feel that praising yourself is silly and useless and way too close to New Age affirmations.

- You can't think of the last time you told yourself, "Good job!"

Learning the language of self-praise may be difficult if your kind words feel stuck in your throat. That is just from lack of practice! The more you try, the easier it is to get the kind words to flow naturally.

Adam's Story

I honestly have trouble finding the words to praise myself when I'm depressed. My brain won't form them. It's not that I don't want to break through and praise myself. I literally *can't*. I find it easy to form words like *failure, worthless, ugly, stupid, lonely, disliked, hated*, and a lot more. But words like *productive, good worker, great colleague, fabulous tennis player*, and *that was fun* just refuse to form. It's like I've had a stroke in the positive words part of my brain.

I now force myself to use positive language, and I say it out loud and rather forcefully. "Good job! I'm so glad you did that, Adam! I'm proud you did that even when you're depressed." It's very uncomfortable, but it's a lot better than the easily formed negative words.

My Story

I spent most of my adult life getting down on myself for being a failure. I never got things done the *right* way. I never met my potential (as so many people so kindly pointed out for 15 years). I was never *enough*. I had thoughts of being ugly and fat, a bad friend, a terrible worker, a dumb decision-maker, a bad singer, a terrible daughter, a rotten partner. Nothing was safe when I was depressed.

I tried to fight this, but really didn't know how. This led to my moving around, changing jobs, and becoming extremely negative when faced with difficult situations. From 1995 until I started to use the strategies in this book, I can't recall very much self-praise. I remember crying a lot and losing friends. I didn't know that I could change my entire life by being nice to myself.

What I do now:

- I'm a lot kinder to myself now. I survived depression, suicidal thoughts, psychosis, sleep issues, and relationship challenges, and I still get out of bed every day. Wow! Good for me!

- I have learned what words are effective, and I pull them out when I feel like I can't: "It's going to be okay, Julie. You're doing your best. You really are! Keep going, Julie. It's going to all work out. You are doing a great job considering what you're going through, Julie."

- This is always a challenge for me as I get caught up in the depression and only see what I don't have and didn't do. I work hard on this now. Daily.

I just finished writing this section, and my brain immediately—and spontaneously—said, "Good for you, Julie!" The self-praise is slow to show up on the dark days, but I still try. Even if I go for days without being able to praise myself the way I want to, I keep trying. Eventually I get there.

Exercise

Please check off the items you've accomplished in your life so far:

- ☐ Had loving relationships
- ☐ Went to school
- ☐ Traveled
- ☐ Finished a project, such as getting active in a group, acting in a play, buying a car, decorating a house, doing well on a work project, etc.
- ☐ Took care of your body
- ☐ Went to work
- ☐ Got out of bed today!
- ☐ Created something beautiful such as a painting or a garden
- ☐ Raised a happy child

Add yours here:

- ☐ _____
- ☐ _____
- ☐ _____

☐ _____

☐ _____

On the bad days, it's really important that *you* are your biggest fan. Others may praise you, but the real praise comes from inside.

ASK DR. PRESTON

Q **Why does it help to praise yourself when you're depressed?**

A People are able to change their moods by way of internal images and self-talk. When you think to yourself, *Look what you did! You screwed up again!* this can, in a potent way, turn up the volume on your depressive feelings. Supportive and encouraging self-talk can do just the opposite. It influences perceptions and helps break through that negative thinking.

You Can Change Your Internal Language

Try this the next time you can only eek out a few movements: "Good job, *(your name here)*!" When you get a project done, "Good job, *(your name here)*! I'm proud of you." Considering the negative voices in your head and the inertia caused by depression, you really are a success if you manage to finish something. Don't discount that. Praise yourself every single time you do something. Say it out loud until it becomes a habit.

Here are some other thoughts to consider:

- If you have a door that's stuck and you really want to get through, you'll keep pushing through that door until you're on the other side. It's the same with praising yourself when you're depressed. Depression makes you stuck; you have to keep going to get through.

- Write *Good for me!* on a sticky note and put it where you can see it. Say "Good for me!" out loud each time you pass the note. Repetition helps you train your brain.

- You don't have to believe everything you say at the beginning, but the more you say it, the more you can believe it.

Remember: Depression will never praise you, but you can praise yourself all day long.

Conclusion

Now that you have 50 strategies to choose from, you're ready to end the hold depression has on your productivity. How do you feel? Hopefully, you can implement a few strategies today. You can then open the book each time you get stuck and try something new. Give yourself time to use them all. I consistently use the 50 strategies to make it through my days. They work!

A FINAL QUESTION FOR DR. PRESTON

Q **What advice do you have for people who have trouble getting things done when they're depressed?**

A It helps to stop struggling against the painful realities of depression and work on accepting your life circumstances as a very difficult yet human experience. Thinking, *This shouldn't happen; it's not fair!* or *What the hell is wrong with me?!* is a common and understandable reaction to the thoughts that occur in the wake of very distressing events. The turning point often occurs when you stop the harsh self-statements and the *should*s and simply say, "I hurt, and I'm sad at what depression does to my life."

This isn't pop psychology, although it has been supported in psychological research. Reframing the negative to something more heartfelt and productive can change the way you view depression in the moment. This is also a part of many spiritual practices. Stopping the struggle against understandable human feelings, combined with developing an attitude of compassion for yourself, is often the key to living with and overcoming depression.

Once you've done that, you can have more energy and enthusiasm to get things done, because you're more able to see that depression does *affect* your life but it doesn't have to *define* your life anymore.

A Final Note from Julie

Two months into writing the book: I woke up depressed today. Before I even got out of bed I had the thought, *What's the point of getting up?* It's hard to feel good about the day and the things you have to get done when your brain is against you from the beginning.

But I knew what I had to do. I said to myself, *I have things to look forward to today, and I'm going to do them. I will not let this thought ruin my day.* (Strategy 16)

I then felt my typical lack of motivation for getting to work, but I reminded myself that motivation is not what gets me to work—I get myself to work. I know I'll feel more motivated once I'm working. In fact, just writing this is already making me feel better. (Strategy 1)

I also knew that driving to my office space would give me a way out if work seemed overwhelming, so I asked my mom to drop me off and pick me up to be sure I'd stay at the office. (Strategy 37)

One problem with working as a writer is the lack of structure. Yes, I have deadlines, but the rest is up to me. No boss looks over my shoulder making sure I get things done. I actually wish I did have someone who could be my taskmaster all day long! When I got to my office, I felt scattered and sad. I had the feeling that I couldn't work today, so I just called up my inner drill sergeant. (Strategy 6)

I also turned off my cell phone. (Strategy 9)

It's so much easier to look at e-mail and chat with friends than do what I have to do. By the time I got to work, I could feel that today was going to be an anxious day if I didn't do something about it immediately. So I reminded myself to breathe and just let my body relax a bit. When I could tell I was going to need more help than my normal treatments, I took a small amount of my antianxiety medication. (Strategies 41 and 45)

I then made out a list of what I had to do and wrote down the times next to each project so I could stay on track. I got out my calendar and made a writing plan for the next two months in order to meet my deadlines. (Strategy 24)

I reminded myself that depression doesn't want me to work, but I want and have to work. (Strategy 14)

It's so hard to stay focused when my mind is all over the place like this, but I remind myself over and over that if I just sit down and work, I will feel *so* much better by the time my mother picks me up that I can truly enjoy my evening. (Strategy 19)

And yes, I do have something to look forward to tonight. I want to be able to enjoy it. Being depressed is hard. It takes a lot of energy to get things done when my brain is not functioning the way I would like it to. When I get to the final chapter edits and feel like I can't continue, I know that this really is a time to think like an athlete. What would a professional athlete do if they had a game to play? They would get out there and do it! (Strategy 10)

So as of this minute, I'm going to work as efficiently as possible and not focus on what I *can't* do. I have a deadline, and I always meet my deadlines. The work might not feel good now, and I might think it's poor writing (Strategy 3), but I know that when the book comes out, I won't be able to tell what I wrote when I was depressed. It will all look good. I won't give up, and I know tomorrow can truly be a better day. (As drill sergeant Scarlet O'Hara would say!)

Present day: You're holding the book in your hand that was so difficult to write on *so* many days. There were days when depression did get the better of me and I couldn't and didn't work, but I still got the project done on time to the best of my ability. There were many days when the strategies looked ridiculous and I wanted to change everything. But I didn't, because I remembered that depression loves to lie to me about these things (Strategy 20) and that I have to keep going. Doing my best is all that I can do when I'm depressed. (Strategy 33)

I'm proud of myself and can honestly say, "Good for you, Julie!" (Strategy 50)

Index

A

accepting
limitations, 217-221
ask Dr. Preston, 221
author's story, 218-219
exercise, 219
losses, 175-179
ask Dr. Preston, 178
author's story, 177
exercise, 178
mom's story, 176-177
ACTH (adrenocorticotropic
hormone), 174
action-oriented therapists, 215
ADHD (attention deficit
hyperactivity disorder), 140
agitated depression, 55
allowing time for positive results,
239-242
ask Dr. Preston, 241
author's story, 240-241
exercise, 241
anxiety, 199-203
author's story, 200-201
brain structures, 202
exercise, 201-202
linking with depression, 202

managing, 202
physical symptoms of
depression, 87
symptoms, 199
artistic creativity, 243-247
ask Dr. Preston, 246
author's story, 244-245
exercise, 245-246
painter's story, 244
asking for help, 117-120
ask Dr. Preston, 120
author's story, 118
exercise, 119
athletic thinking, 49-53
ask Dr. Preston, 52
author's story, 50
baseball player's story, 50
exercise, 51
goal focused, 53
"Just do it!," 49
removing mental thoughts, 53
teamwork, 52
visualizing success, 52
attention deficit hyperactivity
disorder (ADHD), 140
avoiding isolation, 155-158
ask Dr. Preston, 157-158
author's story, 156-157

exercise, 157
signs of, 155
awareness
    ask Dr. Preston, 42
    author's story, 40
    exercise, 41
    overview, 39-40
    self-reminders, 42

B

babysitters, 193
The Beatles' "Revolution #9," 57
best efforts, 159-163
    ask Dr. Preston, 162
    author's story, 160-161
    changing, 159
    exercise, 161-162
    quality of work, 163
brain
    anxiety brain structures, 202
        chatter, 55-58
        agitated depression, 55
        ask Dr. Preston, 57
        author's story, 56-57
        exercise, 57
        interference with making
            decisions, 17-18
        overriding, 20
        recognizing, 55
        reducing, 58
    lying brain, 95-96
        ask Dr. Preston, 98
        author's story, 96-97

exercise, 97-98
    finding truths, 98-99
breaking
    depression barrier, 63-66
        ask Dr. Preston, 65
        author's story, 64
        exercise, 65
    projects into steps, 113-116
        ask Dr. Preston, 116
        author's story, 114-115
        exercise, 115-116

C

caffeine highs, 143-148
    ask Dr. Preston, 147
    author's story, 144-145
    candy example, 144
    exercise, 145-146
    mood fluctuations, 143-144
catatonic depression
    ask Dr. Preston, 42
    author's story, 40
    exercise, 41
    overview, 39-40
    self-reminders, 42
chatter in the brain, 55-58
    agitated depression, 55
    ask Dr. Preston, 57
    author's story, 56-57
    exercise, 57
    interference with making
        decisions, 17-18
    overriding, 20

recognizing, 55
reducing, 58
choosing exercises, 187
circadian rhythm, 105
completing physical tasks, 49-53
    ask Dr. Preston, 52
    author's story, 50
    baseball player's story, 50
    exercise, 51
    goal focused, 53
    "Just do it!," 49
    removing mental thoughts, 53
    teamwork, 52
    visualizing success, 52
conveniences, 193
corticotrophin releasing factor
    (CRF), 108
creating
    feelings of motivation, 4-5
    work spaces, 23
        ask Dr. Preston, 26
        author's story, 24-25
        constantly searching for,
            26-27
        exercise, 25-26
        options, 23-24
        software engineer's story,
            24
creativity, 243-247
    ask Dr. Preston, 246
    author's story, 244-245
    exercise, 245-246
    painter's story, 244
CRF (corticotrophin releasing
    factor), 108

crying, 171-174
    ask Dr. Preston, 173-174
    author's story, 172-173
    exercise, 173
    managing, 174

D

daily life structure, 33-34
    ask Dr. Preston, 36
    author's story, 34-35
    benefits, 36-37
    exercise, 35-36
    importance, 33-34
decision making, 18-21
    ask Dr. Preston, 20
    author's story, 18
    brain interference with, 17-18
    exercise, 19
    guilt, 17
    overriding your brain, 20
delay of gratification, 242
depression
    ADHD, compared, 140
    agitated, 55
    barrier, 63-66
        ask Dr. Preston, 65
        author's story, 64
        exercise, 65
    catatonic
        ask Dr. Preston, 42
        author's story, 40
        exercise, 41
        overview, 39-40
        self-reminders, 42

compared to low self-esteem, 149-153

educating friends/family about, 166-169

ask Dr. Preston, 168

author's story, 166-167

exercise, 167

lack of information, 165-166

nieces/nephews story, 166

lethargic, 55

symptoms, 67

distractions, 43-47

ask Dr. Preston, 46

author's story, 44

exercise, 45-46

doing your best, 159-163

ask Dr. Preston, 162

author's story, 160-161

changing, 159

exercise, 161-162

quality of work, 163

drill sergeant voice, 29-30

ask Dr. Preston, 31

author's story, 30

exercise, 31

remaining positive, 32

E

educating friends/family about depression, 166-169

ask Dr. Preston, 168

author's story, 166-167

exercise, 167

lack of information, 165-166

nieces/nephews story, 166

education. See school

exercise programs, 185-188

amount needed, 185

ask Dr. Preston, 187

author's story, 186

choosing exercises, 187

night before planning, 135

personal trainers, 193

exercises

accepting limitations, 219

anxiety, 201-202

asking for help, 119

awareness, 41

brain chatter, 57

breaking projects into steps, 115-116

caffeine/sugar highs, 145-146

creativity, 245-246

crying, 173

daily life structure, 35-36

decision making, 19

depression barrier, 65

distractions, 45-46

doing your best, 161-162

educating friends/family, 167

finishing projects one at a time, 197

focusing, 9, 129-130

impatience, 241

inner drill sergeant, 31

isolation, 157

judgmental thoughts, 15

lies, 97-98

losses, 178
low self-esteem, 151-152
medications, 225-226
motivation, 3
outside limits, 183
paying for help, 191
physical symptoms of
  depression, 89
procrastination, 103
purpose in work, 231-232
saying no, 123
scheduling, 237
school, 75
self-praise, 251-252
sitting down, 92
sleep, 107
symptoms of depression, 69
talking back to depression,
  81-82
therapist qualities, 213-214
thinking like athletes, 51
thinking problems, 139-140
time limits, 85
watching what you say,
  207-208
work spaces, 25-26
working with friends, 111
writing positive messages, 61

F

family
  asking for help, 117-120
    ask Dr. Preston, 120
    author's story, 118
    exercise, 119

educating about depression,
  166-169
  ask Dr. Preston, 168
  author's story, 166-167
  exercise, 167
  lack of information,
    165-166
  nieces/nephews story, 166
working with, 109-112
  ask Dr. Preston, 111
  author's story, 110
  benefits, 109
  exercise, 111
  suggestions for, 112
  teacher's story, 110
feeling
  the depression, 68-71
    ask Dr. Preston, 70
    author's story, 68
    symptoms exercise, 69
    waking up depressed, 67-68
  oppressive, 63-66
finding
  purpose, 229-233
    ask Dr. Preston, 232
    author's story, 230-231
    exercise, 231-232
  therapists, 211-215
  truths, 98-99
finishing
  projects one at a time, 195-198
    ask Dr. Preston, 197
    author's story, 196
    exercise, 197
    technical writer's story, 196
  school, 76-77

focusing, 127-131
  ask Dr. Preston, 130
  author's story, 128-129
  exercise, 129-130
  goals, 53
  inwardly, 7
  learning, 131
  outwardly, 7-11
    ask Dr. Preston, 10
    author's story, 8
    exercise, 9
    recognition of inward
      focus, 7-8
  on projects one at a time,
    195-198
    ask Dr. Preston, 197
    author's story, 196
    exercise, 197
    technical writer's story, 196
  runner's story, 128
friends
  asking for help, 117-120
    ask Dr. Preston, 120
    author's story, 118
    exercise, 119
  educating about depression,
    166-169
    ask Dr. Preston, 168
    author's story, 166-167
    exercise, 167
    lack of information,
      165-166
    nieces/nephews story, 166
  working with, 109-112
    ask Dr. Preston, 111
    author's story, 110

    benefits, 109
    exercise, 111
    suggestions for, 112
    teacher's story, 110

G–H

goals, 53
guilt in decision making, 17

hiring babysitters, 193
hours in a week, 235-238
  ask Dr. Preston, 238
  author's story, 236-237
  exercise, 237

I

ignoring your internal critic,
  13-16
  ask Dr. Preston, 16
  author's story, 14
  ESL teacher's story, 14
  exercise, 15
  self-praise, 249-252
impatience, 239-241
  ask Dr. Preston, 241
  author's story, 240-241
  exercise, 241
inner drill sergeant, 29-30
  ask Dr. Preston, 31
  author's story, 30
  exercise, 31
  remaining positive, 32

internal critic, 13-16
    ask Dr. Preston, 16
    author's story, 14
    ESL teacher's story, 14
    exercise, 15
    self-praise, 249-252
inward focus, 7
isolation avoidance, 155-158
    ask Dr. Preston, 157-158
    author's story, 156-157
    exercise, 157
    signs of, 155

J–K

judging projects objectively,
    13-16
    ask Dr. Preston, 16
    author's story, 14
    ESL teacher's story, 14
    exercise, 15
jumping between projects, 197
"Just do it!," 49

L

lack of motivation, 1-2
    ask Dr. Preston, 4
    author's story, 3
    exercise, 3
    painter's story, 2
learning focus, 129-131
lethargic depression, 55

letter writing, 59-62
    ask Dr. Preston, 62
    author's story, 60
    exercise, 61
limitations, 181-184, 217-221
    ask Dr. Preston, 183, 221
    author's story, 182-183, 218-219
    exercise, 183, 219
    time, 83-86
        ask Dr. Preston, 85
        author's story, 84-85
        exercise, 85
        physical measurements, 86
losses, 175-179
    ask Dr. Preston, 178
    author's story, 177
    exercise, 178
    mom's story, 176-177
low self-esteem, 149-153
    ask Dr. Preston, 152-153
    author's story, 151
    compared to depression,
        149-153
    exercise, 151-152
lying brain, 95-96
    ask Dr. Preston, 98
    author's story, 96-97
    exercise, 97-98
    finding truths, 98-99

M

making decisions, 18-21
    ask Dr. Preston, 20
    author's story, 18

brain interference with, 17-18
exercise, 19
guilt, 17
overriding your brain, 20
medications, 223-227
  ask Dr. Preston, 226
  author's story, 224-225
  exercise, 225-226
  side effects, 227
memory problems, 137-141
  ask Dr. Preston, 140
  author's story, 138-139
  exercise, 139-140
  fishing guide's story, 138
  signs, 137
mood fluctuations, 143
motivation
  creating, 4-5
  lack of, 1-2
    ask Dr. Preston, 4
    author's story, 3
    exercise, 3
    painter's story, 2
  self-generated, 4

N

night before planning, 133-136
  ask Dr. Preston, 136
  author's story, 134
  exercise, 135
  single dad's story, 134

O

OCD (obsessive-compulsive disorder), 57
oppressive feelings
  ask Dr. Preston, 65
  author's story, 64
  exercise, 65
outside limits, 181-184
  ask Dr. Preston, 183
  author's story, 182-183
  exercise, 183
outward focus, 7-11
  ask Dr. Preston, 10
  author's story, 8
  exercise, 9
  recognition of inward focus, 7-8
overscheduling, 235-238
  ask Dr. Preston, 238
  author's story, 236-237
  exercise, 237

P–Q

paying for
  conveniences, 193
    ask Dr. Preston, 192
    author's story, 190-191
    exercise, 191
    public-relations business story, 190
  help, 189-192
    ask Dr. Preston, 192
    author's story, 190-191

exercise, 191
public-relations business
story, 190
personal trainers, 193
physical symptoms, 87
anxiety, 87
ask Dr. Preston, 90
author's story, 88-89
exercise, 89
signs, 87-88
treating, 90
physical task completion, 49-53
ask Dr. Preston, 52
author's story, 50
baseball player's story, 50
exercise, 51
goal focused, 53
"Just do it!," 49
removing mental thoughts, 53
teamwork, 52
visualizing success, 52
planning days the night before,
133-136
ask Dr. Preston, 136
author's story, 134
exercise, 135
single dad's story, 134
positive messages, 59-62
ask Dr. Preston, 62
author's story, 60
exercise, 61
positive results, 239-242
ask Dr. Preston, 241
author's story, 240-241
exercise, 241

praising yourself, 249-252
ask Dr. Preston, 252
author's story, 250-251
exercise, 251-252
Dr. Preston's advice on
accepting limitations, 221
anxiety brain structures, 202
asking for help, 120
awareness, 42
brain chatter, 57
breaking projects into steps,
116
caffeine/sugar highs, 147
creativity, 246
crying, 173-174
decision making, 20
depression barrier, 65
distractions, 46
doing your best, 162
educating friends/family, 168
exercise programs, 187
feeling the depression, 70
finding truths, 98-99
finishing projects one at a
time, 197
focusing, 130
impatience, 241
inner drill sergeant, 31
isolation, 157-158
judging projects objectively, 16
lies, 98
losses, 178
low self-esteem, 152-153
medications, 226
night before planning, 136

outside limits, 183
physical symptoms of
   depression, 90
procrastination, 103
purpose in work, 232
saying no, 124
scheduling, 238
school, 75
self-generated motivation, 4
self-praise, 252
selfish behaviors, 10
sitting down, 93
sleep problems, 108
spending money for help, 192
structure, 36
talking back to depression, 81
therapy, 214
thinking
   like athletes, 52
   problems, 140
time limits, 85
watching what you say, 208
work spaces, 26
working with friends, 111
writing positive messages, 62
procrastination, 102-104
   ask Dr. Preston, 103
   author's story, 102
   exercise, 103
   making deals with yourself,
      101-102
projects
   asking for help with, 117-120
      ask Dr. Preston, 120
      author's story, 118
      exercise, 119

breaking into steps, 113-116
   ask Dr. Preston, 116
   author's story, 114-115
   exercise, 115-116
doing your best, 159-163
   ask Dr. Preston, 162
   author's story, 160-161
   changing, 159
   exercise, 161-162
   quality of work, 163
finding purpose, 229-233
   ask Dr. Preston, 232
   author's story, 230-231
   exercise, 231-232
finishing one at a time,
   195-198
   ask Dr. Preston, 197
   author's story, 196
   exercise, 197
   technical writer's story, 196
judging objectively, 13-16
   ask Dr. Preston, 16
   author's story, 14
   ESL teacher's story, 14
   exercise, 15
jumping between, 197
outside limits, 181-184
   ask Dr. Preston, 183
   author's story, 182-183
   exercise, 183
overwhelmed by, 113
paying for conveniences, 190
paying for help, 189-193
   ask Dr. Preston, 192
   author's story, 190-191
   exercise, 191

saying no, 121-125
    ask Dr. Preston, 124
    author's story, 122-123
    exercise, 123
    party-planning story, 121-122
    tips, 124-125
working with friends, 109-112
    ask Dr. Preston, 111
    author's story, 110
    benefits, 109
    exercise, 111
    suggestions for, 112
    teacher's story, 110
worrying about finishing, 102-104
    ask Dr. Preston, 103
    author's story, 102
    exercise, 103
    making deals with yourself, 101-102
purpose in work, 229-233
    ask Dr. Preston, 232
    author's story, 230-231
    exercise, 231-232

R

ready-made foods, 193
recognizing
    brain chatter, 55
    focusing inwardly, 7
reducing brain chatter, 58
regulating sleep, 105-108
    ask Dr. Preston, 108
    author's story, 106
disturbers, 107
exercise, 107
tips for restful sleep, 108
removing distractions, 43-47
    ask Dr. Preston, 46
    author's story, 44
    exercise, 45-46
researching therapy styles, 214
restaurants, 193
"Revolution #9," 57

S

saying
    no, 121-125
        ask Dr. Preston, 124
        author's story, 122-123
        exercise, 123
        party-planning story, 121-122
        tips, 124-125
    what you feel, 205-209
schedules, 235-238
    ask Dr. Preston, 238
    author's story, 236-237
    exercise, 237
school
    ask Dr. Preston, 75
    author's story, 74-75
    difficulties, 73-74
    exercise, 75
    finishing, 76-77
    law student's story, 74
    structure, 76

self-esteem, 149-152
    ask Dr. Preston, 152-153
    author's story, 151
    compared to depression,
        149-153
    exercise, 151-152
self-generated motivation, 4
self-praise, 249-252
    ask Dr. Preston, 252
    author's story, 250-251
    exercise, 251-252
selfish behaviors, 7, 10
setting
    outside limits, 181-184
        ask Dr. Preston, 183
        author's story, 182-183
        exercises, 183
    time limits, 83-86
        ask Dr. Preston, 85
        author's story, 84-85
        exercise, 85
        physical measurements, 86
sitting down, 91-94
    ask Dr. Preston, 93
    author's story, 92
    exercise, 92
    representations, 94
sleeping, 105-108
    ask Dr. Preston, 108
    author's story, 106
    disturbers, 107
    exercise, 107
    tips for restful sleep, 108

spending money for
    conveniences, 193
        ask Dr. Preston, 192
        author's story, 190-191
        exercise, 191
        public-relations business
            story, 190
    help, 189-193
        ask Dr. Preston, 192
        author's story, 190-191
        exercise, 191
        public-relations business
            story, 190
stress hormone, 174
structure
    daily life, 33-34
        ask Dr. Preston, 36
        author's story, 34-35
        benefits, 36-37
        exercise, 35-36
        importance, 33-34
    planning days the night
        before, 133-136
        ask Dr. Preston, 136
        author's story, 134
        exercise, 135
        single dad's story, 134
    school, 76
sugar highs, 143-148
    ask Dr. Preston, 147
    author's story, 144-145
    candy example, 144
    exercise, 145-146
    mood fluctuations, 143-144

symptoms of depression, 67-69
  anxiety, 87
  ask Dr. Preston, 90
  author's story, 88-89
  exercise, 89
  signs, 87-88
  treating, 90

T–U–V

talking
  back to depression, 79-80
    ask Dr. Preston, 81
    author's story, 80
    exercise, 81-82
  watching what you say, 205-209
    ask Dr. Preston, 208
    author's story, 206-207
    exercise, 207-208
tasks. *See* projects
teamwork, 52
therapy, 193, 211-215
  action-oriented therapists, 215
  ask Dr. Preston, 214
  author's story, 212-213
  benefits, 214
  finding therapists, 211-215
  researching, 214
  therapist qualities exercise, 213-214
thinking
  like athletes, 49-53
    ask Dr. Preston, 52
    author's story, 50

    baseball player's story, 50
    exercise, 51
    goal focused, 53
    "Just do it!," 49
    removing mental thoughts, 53
    teamwork, 52
    visualizing success, 52
  problems with, 137-141
    ask Dr. Preston, 140
    author's story, 138-139
    exercise, 139-140
    fishing guide's story, 138
    signs, 137
  in steps, 113-116
    ask Dr. Preston, 116
    author's story, 114-115
    exercise, 115-116
thoughts
  focusing, 127-131
    ask Dr. Preston, 130
    author's story, 128-129
    exercise, 129-130
    learning, 131
    runner's story, 128
  judgmental, 13-16
    ask Dr. Preston, 16
    author's story, 14
    ESL teacher's story, 14
    exercise, 15
  lies, 95-96
    ask Dr. Preston, 98
    author's story, 96-97
    exercise, 97-98
    finding truths, 98-99

time
  allowing positive results,
    239-242
    ask Dr. Preston, 241
    author's story, 240-241
    exercise, 241
  limits, 83-86
    ask Dr. Preston, 85
    author's story, 84-85
    exercise, 85
    physical measurements, 86
  overscheduling, 235-238
    ask Dr. Preston, 238
    author's story, 236-237
    exercise, 237

visualizing success, 52

W–X–Y–Z

waking up depressed, 67-68
watching what you say, 205-209
  ask Dr. Preston, 208
  author's story, 206-207
  exercise, 207-208
work spaces, 23
  ask Dr. Preston, 26
  author's story, 24-25
  constantly searching for, 26-27
  exercise, 25-26
  options, 23-24
  software engineer's story, 24
working out. See exercise
  programs

working with
  family/friends, 109-112
    ask Dr. Preston, 111
    author's story, 110
    benefits, 109
    exercise, 111
    suggestions for, 112
    teacher's story, 110
  teams, 52
worrying factor, 102-104
  ask Dr. Preston, 103
  author's story, 102
  exercise, 103
  losing, 104
  making deals with yourself,
    101-102
writing positive messages, 59-62
  ask Dr. Preston, 62
  author's story, 60
  exercise, 61